For Jane Taylor
... with my
appreciation of
your beautiful life
these past 50 years!

Donald S. Pady
April 20, 2004

POETRY OF

WILLIAM ALLEN WHITE

Collected and Edited by
Donald Stuart Pady

LEATHERS
PUBLISHING

A division of Squire Publishers, Inc.
4500 College Blvd.
Leawood, KS 66211
1/888/888-7696

Copyright 2002
Printed in the United States

ISBN: 1-58597-156-1 (Soft cover)
ISBN: 1-58597-149-9 (Hard cover)

Library of Congress Control Number: 2002106818

Printings: 1 2 3 4 5 6 7 8 9

A division of Squire Publishers, Inc.
4500 College Blvd.
Leawood, KS 66211
1/888/888-7696

In the Poet's Belated Book

I bring these rhymes, but had I brought a rose instead,

It would have withered ere the day I chose was dead.

Full many a rose blooms — tho' a wi'hered thing — thro years,

In other roses for the thoughts they bring and tears.

Let these rhymes live when some clear voice shall try my themes,

I had his hopes one time, and e'en had I his dreams.

(Kansas City Star, May 20, 1894)

CONTENTS

PREFACE

I became acquainted with several reporters and editors of *The Emporia Gazette* while a graduate student in Library Science at Emporia State University between 1961 and 1962. They sometimes talked about anxious moments when their newspaper copy faced deadlines and irritable editors. Sagging subscriptions, rising costs of paper and inks, and the constant pressure to get enough advertising, seemed like only a few problems always present in a small-town, daily newspaper. Occasionally I asked them about the history of the *Gazette* and what it was like to have worked for the late editor, William Allen White. Their answers invariably pointed with pride to the *Gazette's* reputation as one of the best-known papers in the Midwest. This reputation, they claimed, was the direct result of White's journalistic philosophy and hard work.

Ted F. McDaniel, then managing editor, had worked with White, and casually told me that White also wrote good poetry. Ted recited and later wrote a short verse about Senator Charles Curtis of Kansas which White had written and published almost 38 years before.[1] I tried to find more examples of White's poetry, and soon discovered that he had published verse and prose-poems in almost every newspaper for which he had worked. I published a brief list of his poems that I had found,[2] but later learned that he had published a great many more. In addition, many poems were located in collections in manuscript — which had not been published.

After his death in 1944, White's correspondence and manuscripts were sorted by Sallie and their son, William Lindsay White. Most were given to the Library of Congress Manuscript Division. Nelson R. Burr, a former member of the General Reference and Bibliography Division of the Library of Congress, summarized the contents of the large collection of approximately 137,000 items totaling 198 linear feet. Burr acknowledged, however, that some of White's files had remained in Kansas, where they were given by the Whites to Kansas institutions which had taken "an active interest in her husband's life and work."[3]

Emporia State University's William Allen White Library was named as one of several repositories for many of White's letters and other materials about Kansas and Kansans — including the extant poetry which White had thought necessary to save. But White had not saved all of his published and unpublished verse. During the next 35 years I collected, verified and explicated his poetry by reading both physical and microfilm copies of books, journals and newspapers in which his poetry appeared. Sources of published poetry are noted after each poem, and unpublished verses are also noted with the manuscript's or typescript's present-day location.

This book contains what the compiler and editor thinks is a complete collection of White's poetry. Poems are arranged chronologically by broad subjects, and will illustrate to the reader how White's thoughts, poetical expressions and styles changed over the years. Textual integrity of the poems has been preserved except where obvious typographical errors in contemporary spelling and grammatical usage have been corrected. The official article, *The,* before *Emporia Gazette* is omitted in poetry citations for the sake of brevity — as is *Daily,* which appeared at various times between *Emporia* and *Gazette.* But if someone discovers a poem by White that has not yet been found, I will gladly accept its inclusion into the collection.

I am grateful to Ms. Barbara White Walker, senior editor of *The Emporia Gazette,* for permission to reprint her grandfather's poetry as it appeared in this newspaper and those published or unpublished poems currently located in the William Allen White Collection in the William Allen White Library of Emporia (Kansas) State University. While the White collection is actually owned by the White family, readers' access to it was superbly provided for 22 years by ESU's Special Collections Librarian, Ms. Mary E. Bogan, now Reference Librarian in the same library since 2001.

I wish to thank the hard-working reference librarians of the Kansas State Historical Society and Washburn University, both in Topeka, and the State Historical Society of Missouri, in Columbia, for access to newspapers on microfilm and a great number of reference materials. Becky Schults, Lawanna Huslig and Lin Fredericksen of the Kansas Collection at the Spencer Research Library of the University of Kansas provided timely assistance in support of my queries about White's verse. Book, newspaper and journal permissions to reprint his poems follow each appropriate poem in its textual notes.

My wife, Carol L. Tulloss Pady, deserves far more credit than I can express; and it is to her that I dedicate my own portion of this book for her patience and support.

PREFATORY NOTES

1 Ted F. McDaniel to D.S. Pady, August 27, 1962; see poem, "Kansas on Guard."

2 Donald S. Pady, "A Bibliography of the Poems of William Allen White," *Bulletin of Bibliography* 25 (2) January-April 1967, 44-46.

3 Nelson R. Burr, "The Papers of William Allen White," The Library of Congress *Quarterly Journal of Current Acquisitions* 4 (1) November 1946, 14. See also, Library of Congress, Manuscript Division, Research Department, *William Allen White; a register and index of his papers in the Library of Congress,* Washington, DC, 1978, no. 52. Available from the Manuscript Division, Library of Congress, Washington, DC 20540.

INTRODUCTION

On the day that William Allen White became editor and owner of the *Emporia Daily Gazette,* William Yost Morgan introduced White to its readers as a poet and journalist. Morgan was the previous editor and owner, and his announcement hailed White as "a good fellow," and that after he had "been in Emporia six weeks everybody will call him 'Bill,' slap him on the back and say, 'We're glad you came.' "[1] For almost 49 years White lived up to Morgan's claim, and became one of the best small-town newspaper editors in the United States.

White also excelled as a novelist, biographer, politician and political advisor, letter-writer and book reviewer. But, unknown to many people, he also wrote poetry. His verse was unusual enough to attract attention even though he merely remembered it as a youthful experiment.[2] While the quality of White's poetry rose far above his modest claim, he admitted that he could better compose more lofty thoughts in rhyme. His poetry usually expressed his eagerness for happy excitement, and was an honest reflection of his strongly determined will.

He admired James Whitcomb Riley, Eugene Field, Hamlin Garland and Will Carleton, and was a personal friend of many other Midwestern writers and poets, including Eugene Fitch "Ironquill" Ware, Edgar Watson Howe and Albert Bigelow Paine. These writers characterized the literature and poetry of the Midwest and the indigenous growth of the prairie. For faithful realism blended with sentiment, White specialized his subjects and characters to get local color. He was close to the soil in time and in feeling, and the mellow haze of atmosphere with which he embodied the mythical region of "Willer Crick" became a shining token of White's fertile imagination. By the critical standards of White's contemporary poets, excellent rhymes and musical rhythms were found throughout the different themes that came to his hand. Some of his poems are full of editorial content; others vividly illustrate the humor, satire and pathos of early Kansas life as seen from the vantage ground of a journalist's consciousness and quick observation.

White was born at Emporia, Kansas, on February 10, 1868, at 628 Merchant Street — the son of Dr. Allen White (1819-1882), a country merchant and physician, and Mary Ann Hatten White (1830-1924), a pioneer school teacher, whom he married April 15, 1867. In 1878 the family moved to El Dorado, Kansas, where William completed high school in 1884. He dabbled in poetry at an early age, but soon discovered how hard it was to compose intelligible verse. He attended the College of Emporia between 1884 and the spring semester of 1886 — where he also learned to set type for T.P. Fulton's *Emporia Daily News.* White returned briefly to El Dorado in the summer of 1885 to become a reporter and compositor for the *Butler County Democrat.* He also reported for the *El Dorado Republican* in 1886 under the guiding influence of the editor and owner, Thomas Benton "Bent" Murdock. From the fall of 1886 to January 1890, White attended the University of Kansas (then named Kansas State University) in Lawrence, where he took a wide variety of liberal arts studies. He reported and edited university news to the *Lawrence Journal* and published several poems in the popular student journal, *University Review.* White's first published book was a compilation of poems by various KU faculty, entitled *Sunflowers,*[3] which he co-edited with Thomas Francis Doran.

Newspaper work so attracted White that he left university before completing requirements for graduation and became assistant editor and business manager of the *El Dorado Republican* in the fall of 1890. "Bent" Murdock hired him to manage the paper while the editor and Kansas senator was on the codifying committee of the Senate and chased political news around eastern Kansas. "Bent" also wrote poetry and published unsigned verses on his editorial page. White followed his example and instructed the compositors to insert his own poems at the top of the editorial page — and to sign his authorship with such forms of his name as "Will A. White," "W.A.W.," "William Allen White," or with his more popular pseudonym, "Elder Twiggs."

White frequently assigned his pseudonym, "Elder Twiggs," to news items, social squibs and poems alike. This sobriquet provided him more anonymity when he poked humorous and satirical jabs at local, county and state officials (or local events), with startling candor. Both his editorials and poetry about the actions of some people — especially about budding romances among single townspeople — occasionally caused hard feelings against him. As early as 1890 some of White's seemingly caustic and satirical remarks in both editorials and poems brought vitriolic reactions from some readers who did not share his views. One poem, submitted in angry retaliation by one "Deacon Simps of the Upper Slate," hotly contested White's editorial position by scolding the assistant editor with a verse entitled, "Some words to Elder Twiggs."[4]

White's poetry praised rustic scenery, and it exemplified the Kansas people who enjoyed their lives and endured common hardships. He called El Dorado "the gayest of all Kansas small towns ..."[5] The Walnut River energized this country town because of all the scenic places for social gatherings along its banks. Boating, fishing, hiking, swimming, picnicking and winter skating entertained countless numbers of people. Boat rental cost only 25¢ per hour and provided an enjoyable way to spend leisure time. There was a mile-long, natural cave about six miles south of town and a waterfall only a few miles out. White loved the Walnut River, and he renamed it "Willow Creek" or "Willer Crick" as the setting of many poems. In an essay entitled "The Boom in Willow Creek,"[6] he described his memories of El Dorado and its growth on the Kansas prairie.

But the young assistant editor was restless, and he confided to a former girlfriend whom he had dated during his years at KU:

> I am now to decide whether I am to be a literary man pure and simple: a city journalist with a department or a country editor with a local political influence and a predilection toward poetry. If I could do what I want to do, I should write poetry, novels — especially novels — (and especially poetry) and have, say, three thousand a year to live on. That is my ideal of a successful man."[7]

This letter predicted his future profession, and he soon found that he could combine a literary and journalistic career. And poetry would become a natural extension of his chosen vocation. Around November 1891 White moved to Kansas City, Missouri, where he was hired to write editorials for the *Kansas City Journal*. His poems periodically appeared on the editorial page, and during this time he was assigned to Topeka, Kansas, as a contributing correspondent for the same newspaper. White's distance from Kansas City may have provided him with a certain amount of physical safety because he sent some scathing poetry about local ward politics and the bosses who controlled the Kansas City elections. He appreciated the political stance of the *Journal* as an independent Republican voice that was willing to support the better candidates of either Republican or Democratic party. But White was compelled to write editorials about special-interest groups in and around Kansas City, and he could not adhere to the prevailing editorial policy that insisted upon restraint to the point of timidity.[8] He angrily resigned from the paper in August 1892 because its telegraph editor placed an important story, which White and an associate had filed from Topeka, among the back-paged market reports in a shortened and revised version. White knew that their story should have scooped front-page space, and this blow to his professional pride forced him to consider other newspapers where there would be fewer controls over his creative, journalistic style.

White quickly joined the staff of the *Kansas City Star*, where he was hired by William Rockhill Nelson to be an editor, short-story writer and poet. He was on the staff from September 1892 to June 1895, and he quickly learned how to editorialize against special interests like corrupt law practices, utility monopolies and poor home- and street-building controls. In addition to his editorial-page column named "Kansas Notes," White often wrote lengthy biographies of regional political figures in the *Star's* supplemental "Extra Sheet," and short stories like "An Assyrian on Willer Crick,"[9] reviews of music and drama — and a number of his own poems. Since he was also the poetry editor, he could control the number and quality of poems contributed to the *Star.* He often pre-empted poems by William Cullen Bryant, Ella Wheeler Wilcox, Oliver Wendell Holmes, Thomas Bailey Aldrich, and the popular Kansas City favorite, Albert Bigelow Paine. White's own verse generally appeared on those days when he restricted the printing of poetry by others.

Paine and White had been friends for several years before their paths crossed in Kansas City, and they had corresponded from their respective homes in the Kansas towns of Fort Scott and El Dorado. They combined their talents to publish the best of their poems in a small book entitled *Rhymes by Two Friends.*[10] Ewing Herbert, formerly joint editor of the Hiawatha (Kansas) *Brown County World,*[11] wrote the book's introduction and observed that there was "no Greek or Latin flavor to their poetry"; their verses recalled the "memories we love — the sound of a voice, the smile of a face, the touch of a hand. They appeal to the heart and soften the hard places in the struggle for life."[12]

Paine published 81 poems in the front portion of the book and financed payment to M.L. Izor of Fort Scott for the private printing of 500 copies. White's 37 poems followed to complete the volume. What happened next, however, prompted White to break his friendship with Paine for many years to come. Both poets were each to receive 100 copies from the printing run for personal distribution or reviewers from various newspapers and periodicals. But Paine took White's allotment and mailed most of them to other reviewers and his own friends — leaving White with none to donate to other poets, reviewers and friends.[13] Disappointed as he must have been, White had no further interest in publishing another book with Paine. Both men had earlier planned to publish a book of short stories, entitled *Sketches by Two Friends*[14] immediately after the issuance of *Rhymes.* But no bibliographical evidence proves its eventual publication, and White's short stories, which would likely have been those to appear in *Sketches,* were probably the same ones as those which later appeared in White's *The Real Issue* (1896). These stories were "entirely his own ... written for the *El Dorado Republican,* the *Kansas City Star* and the *Emporia Gazette.*"[15]

White's deep regret over Paine's selfish action caused him to think seriously about the underlying reasons why poets create lines of verse in the first place. His initial humiliation and regret over the Paine incident slowly subsided. At the same time, White's growing maturity filled him with resolution and self-determination to become a better poet. His short essay, "Concerning 'Art for Art's Sake,'" portrayed his belief about the theory and practice of poetry. He thought that there was "no such thing as art for art's sake," but rather, "true art is for the heart's sake." If true poetry were to be understood by the average man, White claimed, it could not depend on the use of fixed rhymes, meters or rules which guided such poets as Wordsworth, Longfellow, Tennyson and others. Poetry was the language of the heart, not solely of the mind, because the "heart speaks to heart through time, through space, through foreign accents on the tongue ..." Contemporary poets like Thomas Bailey Aldrich and James Whitcomb Riley, White thought, sang as brothers of all men because they were recorders of the human heart. Naturally, the topics of human subjects opened poetic access to the democracy of the human heart, whereas the academic aristocracy of the human mind turned White against the

ethereal, unreal, often unintelligible, and too frequently inane, expression of no common brotherhood, acknowledged aristocracy, appealing to a class, and promulgating theories of unusual ... mental and emotional development.

White's theory of poetic expression thus formed the standard of poetry he pledged to follow. He insisted on poetic truth as it was revealed in real-life situations of the heart. "Write of the joys of earth," he said:

Write in human blood of human things, plainly, and with directness that may not be misunderstood; write every line for every man, write neither up nor down, but to the level of the universal heart.[16]

Soon after taking over the *Emporia Gazette* on June 1, 1895, however, White found that the day-to-day business of editing and managing a small-town newspaper was his main concern. National and local politics, literature, music, drama, poetry — and his many other interests in the pursuit of happiness in his marriage — only formed a corona around his central source of energy. Under his editorship the appearance of poetry in the *Gazette* almost stopped, except for a few of his own poems that occasionally revealed themselves. He had to rebuild the paper's subscription base, to solicit more advertising, and to use every column-inch of available space for well-reported news items. In retrospect, one can examine any of the 718 weekly newspapers printed in Kansas in 1892 to see examples of how much poetry was printed. Obituary verse that praised the life of the recently departed frequently accompanied death notices on every page; poems of every rhyme, meter and topic were tombstoned between local news stories and commercial advertisements. Even badly written poetry was used as "filler" so that no blank space would glare uncomfortably at the reader. As critic O.E. Olin noted:

> His principal work in the future will undoubtedly be in the line of prose. He says that he has taken "the cure" for poetry, but its entire success may be doubted. He has lived close to Nature, and she has whispered many things and we shall expect him some time to tell us in Nature's own rhythmic way.[17]

White discovered that *Gazette* readers enjoyed his poetry regardless of the quality, or lack of it. Once, when announcing in the paper of an early-office closing on Independence Day — so that the staff could put the *Gazette* to bed before noon and enjoy the rest of the holiday at home ... he quipped, "With these few brief remarks the entire *Gazette* force joins the office devil in proclaiming:

> Here's to the American eagle,
> Proud bird of freedom all hail;
> The fowl whom none can inveigle,
> Or put salt on its beautiful tail.[18]

Since the poem was unsigned, *Gazette* readers probably thought that it *was* the office devil who composed it. The editor's skill in putting his own thoughts and words into the actions expected of his employees marked his managerial technique of directing human motivation. And White certainly understood the value of verse as a commercial advertisement. He often wrote clever jingles for several stores in Emporia. One stated that "Little Jack ain't the only one who is surprised at the quality of goods and the lowness of prices at the 5 & 10¢ store ...":

> Little Jack Horner
> Sat in the corner
> Wondering what he should buy;
> Then he opened the door
> Of the 5 and 10¢ store,
> And almost dropped dead with a sigh.
> It was all so cheap
> That he fell in a heap
> And wished that his dimes were all dollars,

For he said, "I know
Every cent I would blow
Buying presents for teachers and scholars."[19]

White even told his typesetters to arrange this poem within attractive borders to tell why readers should subscribe to the *Gazette:*
Come to Emporia,
Make no delay.
See in the *Gazette*
We show you the way.[20]

The decision over whether or not to print poetry contributed by others was clearly stated on the editorial page of February 13, 1901. White posted a small notice that the *Gazette* would print poetry once per year. This new policy undoubtedly stopped or slowed the large quantity of poems sent to the editor by everyone who thought they had something to say in verse. The traditional custom of printing obituary poetry bothered White enough to later exclaim, "The worst poetry in the world is that which is inspired by the death of some friend or relative." He thought obituary poems were "so wretchedly, insufferably bad, that the people in whose memory they were written must be weeping in heaven."[21] Yet, White never said flatly that he would not print his own poetry; he simply meant that the appearance of any poem would be controlled by the editor — and at his discretion. He again headed his editorial column on April 27, 1901 with the disclaimer that although "the *Gazette* has an iron-clad rule against poetry, once a year this paper violates this rule to print James Whitcomb Riley's "When the green gets back in the trees.'"

White never stopped writing poetry, however, but several reasons probably caused the hiatus in his otherwise frequent poetry production in the *Gazette.* He hired Walt Mason (1862-1939) in 1907 to write news articles and editorials. Mason also excelled in writing prose poems, which contemporary journalists called "machine poetry." White had occasionally written "machine poetry" in years past, but he probably felt that Mason's daily column in prose verse was enough for *Gazette* readers without adding his own poetry as possible competition to Mason's. "Upon occasion," wrote Rolla A. Clymer, both White and Mason "would collaborate in blocking out display heads in rhyme — the main and decks and sub-decks all forming a true jingle."[22] A good example appeared in the *Gazette* on the front page of the November 18, 1907 issue: "Corn shellers rattle and hay presses churn; the thrashers and cider mills hump; Chicago is turning out money to burn; Get a tub and stand under the dump."

Another one, on the previous day, when Oklahoma statehood was officially announced, went like this: "So here's to you, Oklahoma, come in take a seat; you are no longer 'Company,' So don't forget to wash your face and keep your fingers neat." Despite the fun both men had in composing these display heads in rhyme, White graciously called Mason the "Poet Laureate of American Democracy."[23]

Another important reason why White's poetry production slowed during the early years of the 20th century was because his fiction writing flourished instead. The encouraging success of *The Real Issue* (1896), *The Court of Boyville* (1899, containing four poems), *Stratagems and Spoils: Stories of Love and Politics* (1901), *In Our Town* (1906) and *A Certain Rich Man* (1909) pointed to his growing popularity as a novelist. Instead of writing occasional verse for the limited readership of the *Emporia Gazette,* he found that he could easily compose and insert poetic devices among the pages of his books — in order to emphasize, speed up or slow down the reader's reaction to the story's progress. White's insertion of a poem to catalyze the story with a "quoted" verse from the fictitious newspaper, *Sycamore Ridge Banner* of September 12, 1867, portrayed the romantic character of Watts McHurdie:

> Hail and farewell to thee, friend of my youth:
> Pilgrim who seekest the Fountain of Truth,
> Hail and farewell to thy innocent pranks,
> No more can I send thee for left-handed cranks.
> Farewell, and a tear laves the ink on my pen,
> For ne'er shall I 'noint thee with strap-oil again.[24]

Whether in book or newspaper format, White wrote poetry about the way of life in Kansas and the United States which was different than the kind of life that we know today. And yet, his poems are for the universal heart — regardless of time or place. His verse describes his experiences, observations and imagination about life as he interpreted it. His poetry expressed a moral tension between the authority of America and the conflicts of American ideals. This tension between rigidness and changing moral idealism was due in some ways to the burgeoning growth of Brother Jonathan — the humorous name of White's United States. In 1900 the U.S. population was 75,994,575, and more than 3,687,000 immigrants were admitted during the previous ten-year period. President Cleveland had vetoed literacy tests for immigrants in 1897, and by the turn of the century, one in ten U.S. adults could not read nor write. The average wage in the U.S. was 22¢ per hour, and the average worker earned between $200 and $400 annually. In 1900 only six percent of all Americans were high school graduates; there were about 230 annually reported murders in the U.S.; marijuana, heroin and morphine were available over drugstore counters. More than 95 percent of all births in the U.S. took place at home. There were only 8,000 automobiles in the entire country and only 144 miles of paved roads. The maximum speed limit in most cities was 10 miles per hour. White noticed and wrote about change and how fast-changing times affected his neighbors.

For nearly 20 years the *Gazette* had taken an abbreviated Associated Press news service, but on March 20, 1922, White announced that the paper would pay $5,000 per year for the AP's full-leased wire service. The resulting increase in national, international and regional news precluded much of the editorial space available to the editor's articles and poems. And especially during hard economic times, White's poetry seemed out of place in a paper which needed more advertising for the financial survival of the paper. Thus, very little of White's poetry appeared after 1922.

White spoke the language of the average American with the authority of one who wanted to make people comfortable in their culture. His personal qualities reflected an inspirational power which helped to give people a sense of direction. Of all the values common to the human masses, White believed that Americans were morally obligated to think clearly about affairs beyond their daily lives. His spoken and written words were guided by his dominant interest — the development of a better and more conscious citizenship. It was this journalist and poet from Emporia who showed people how to discover and extend their reaches into the arena of public spirit.

Donald Stuart Pady, M.S., M.A.

INTRODUCTORY NOTES

[1] William Yost Morgan, "Bill White," *Emporia Daily Gazette,* June 1, 1895, and *The Weekly Gazette,* June 6, 1895. He married Sallie Moss Lindsay, a Kansas City, Missouri school teacher, April 27, 1893. White died in Emporia on January 29, 1944 — ironically, on "Kansas Day."

[2] White's first poem, located in a notebook which his mother had saved for him, was entitled, "Whatever is, is right."

[3] *Sunflowers; poems written by various hands in the State University of Kansas.* ed. Thomas Francis Doran and William Allen White. Lawrence, Kansas: Journal Publishing Co., 1888. Doran (1862-1939) was an 1888 graduate of K.S.U. and went on to practice law in Topeka from 1891 until his death.

[4] "Some words to Elder Twiggs," *El Dorado Republican,* April 25, 1890, p. 3, The Upper Slate River was located northwest of Hamilton in Greenwood County, Kansas.

[5] "Over in Kansas," *Kansas City Journal,* July 15, 1892.

[6] *Walnut Valley Times,* March 8, 1895, p. 6.

[7] White to Helen Sutliff, January 21, 1891. Courtesy Stanford University Library, Department of Special Collections and Archives.

[8] For an expanded account, see Walter Johnson, ed., *Selected letters of William Allen White, 1899-1942.* New York: Henry Holt, 1947, 5.

[9] *Kansas City Star,* March 9, 1893, 5.

[10] Albert Bigelow Paine and William Allen White, *Rhymes by Two Friends.* Illustrations by Hannah Heine and M.A. Waterman. Fort Scott, Kansas: Printing done with fidelity by M.L. Izor & Son, 1893. The Introduction is dated August 15, 1893.

[11] Ewing Herbert was joint editor with Daniel W. Wilder (1832-1911).

[12] Paine and White, op. cit., iv.

[13] Albert Bigelow Paine, "Rhymes by Two Friends; the story of a Kansas book," *Kansas Magazine,* 2 (September 1909), 65-66. "M.L. Izor sold what he could of his 300 of the first printing, but then turned the remainder over to Paine to satisfy the amount advanced. Thus Paine became the publisher, but he didn't make anything, did not come out even."

[14] Scarcely noticeable in *Rhymes by Two Friends* is a publisher's advertisement located between the *verso* of the first unnumbered leaf following page 228 and the two succeeding terminal endpapers: (Line changes are marked with slashes)
Sketches by TWO FRIENDS (in press)/
Edition limited to 500 copies/
Price, $1./
Being a collection of short stories and sketches of Western life by ALBERT/ BIGELOW PAINE and William/ Allen White./ A number of these stories have appeared from time to time in various leading/ magazines and newspapers through/ out the country, attracting general attention by their realistic and vigorous delineation of life and its humors, its/pathos and its tragedies. They are/ now collected and published, with a/ number of others not before in print./ M.L. Izor & Son/ Fort Scott, Kansas.

[15] Joe W. Kraus, "The Publication of William Allen White's *The Real Issue,*" *Kansas Historical Quarterly* 43 (2), Summer 1977, 193-202. Published with permission.

[16] William Allen White, "Concerning 'Art for Art's Sake,'" *The Agora* 3 (4), 1894, 290-95.

[17] O.E. Olin, "Will White — Boy and Man," *Western Homes* I (October 1897), 12-14.

[18] *Emporia Gazette,* July 4, 1895.

[19] *Emporia Gazette,* November 21, 1900. White wrote an earlier, unsigned, commercial jingle in the *Gazette,* December 7, 1895, p.1, for Jones & Sons, 517 Commercial, Emporia, entitled, "The Best Dressed Man in Town."

[20] *Emporia Gazette,* March 18, 1899. Other examples of White's commercial poems of early 1901 plugged a front-page advertisement for Peters Hardware Company.

[21] *Emporia Gazette,* December 13, 1907.

[22] Rolla A. Clymer, "Thomas Benton Murdock and William Allen White," *Kansas Historical Quarterly* 23 (3) Autumn 1957, 255. Published with permission.

[23] Kansas State Historical Society and Department of Archives, *History of Kansas Newspapers* ... Topeka: Kansas State Printing Plant, 1916, 114.

[24] William Allen White, *A Certain Rich Man,* New York: Macmillan, 1909, 57. White also inserted song lyrics to emphasize vocal, tonal and changing moods of his fictional characters; see also p. 126.

WILLER CRICK

A Twelfth Month Idyl

Everything a freezin' up, 'long about December;
Willer Crick amongst the rest, 'f I don't disremember,
Froze up tighter 'n a brick, 'ceptin' where Bill Olkum
Throwed a whoppin' rock er stick, "t' see if it 'ud hold him";
Slick ez glass an' green an' thick, temptin' an' a-teasin';
Hear it poppin' up the crick while it's still a-freesin';
Hear the clinkin' of the skates, comin' thro' the timber —
Nosey Jim an' Shorty Bates[1] 'll soon be gittin' limber.
I kin say now I've begun, " 'f I don't disremember,
Willer Crick's the place fer fun, 'long about December."

Build a big ol' driftwood fire, sizzlin' an' a-smokin',
Fer the gals to stand around, shiv'rin' an' a chokin',
Till their fellers prances in, with some quirl erruther,
Sayin': "Shan't we try agin; go a little futher,
Up the slew er round the ben', 'way from where the crowd is,"
Er some sich like words — an' then — well, you know jes' how 't is —
Fer you orto see the ice, Satterdays an' sich days:
Looks jes' like a nest of mice, runnin' ev'ry which ways.
Ar debatin' club looks sick, fer 'bout ev'ry member
Sneaks off down to Willer Crick, 'long about December.

Afternoons when school is out, 'bout a hundred fellers,
Rat'lin skates and dinner pails, headed by Jack Sellers,
Comes a-pilin' down the bank, an' before you know it
Give their straps a twistin' yank, an' away they go it —
Some a-cuttin' curlycues, some a-playin' shinny,[2]
Some a-runnin' like the duce[3] after likklt Skinny
Johnson, who's a being "it" in some game erruther;
Cross tag, mebbe — I fergit — can't tell which from tuther;
But they're having fun, you bet, more'n in September,
Fur they don't get overhet, 'long about December.

Then the fellers with their girls, haint they more'n happy —
Girls 'ith cheeks an' lips so red, and 'ith eyes so snappy —
Skatin' up an' skatin' down, dodgin' folks 'at pass you;
Skatin' where they's no 'un "roun," no 'un to harass you.

Willer Crick boys wa'nt' much good, 't raising' Ned[4] and larkin',[5]
But you bet they usta could beat the world a-sparkin'.
They's a piece I heard tell of, says 'at young men's fancies
Lightly turns to thoughts o' love, in the spring; the chances
Are the reason this was sed, is 'at we remember
In the spring the fun we've hed 'long about December.

(*University Review,* University of Kansas, X No. 4, December 1888, 102; Hattie Horner, compiler, *Collection of Kansas Poetry,* Topeka, Kansas, 1891. • 1. Probably Shorty Bates of El Dorado, Kansas; see also "Shorty" in the group of poems entitled Newspaperdom. • 2. Hockey, as played by schoolboys using a curved stick. • 3. Deuce; the devil. • 4. raising Ned; up to mischief. • 5. larking; to sport or frolic.)

——

The Ol' Wood Pump

They's differ'nt things about a farm 'at takes a feller's eye;
Some think 'at pigs is pickchuresk, though durned if I see why;
An' others thinks 'at bleating sheep an' wobbly -legged colts
Is proper things fer folk to paint, but that jest somehow jolts
On my artistic feelin's, bein' raised, y' understand,
On "Rock of Ages," "Plate of Fruit," an' "Views from Holy Land."
But speakin' of yer music, now I guess you hav' to hump,
If you beat the laffin' gurgle of
                                        the ol'
                                              wood
                                                    pump.

It used to stand behind the house right near the ellum tree,
Though summers 't was not shaded much it didn't seem to me,
Fer afternoons it was so hot it jest 'ud burn yer feet —
I mean the platform 'ud; an' then you never saw the beat
Of how it lickt the wotter up before you'd pumped a spell,
An' my! but wa'n't the wotter cool from way down in the well;

4

You most could taste the coolness, an' yer taster'd give a jump
To meet the wotter bubblin' in

the ol'

wood

pump.

The han's 'ud wash there mornin's, an' the stock 'ud come at night,
To drink ez fast ez Lige could pump an' work 'ith all his might.
The cattle they'd injoy it, though, an' when they'd got enuff
They'd stick their noses in the troft an' pull 'em out an' snuff,
So when the stock 'ud go away, an' Lige was perty hot
He'd stop the spout a runnin' 'ith his hand, ez like ez not;
He'd pump a bit, then shut his eyes, an' put his mouth down plump,
An' drink a stream of gladness from

the ol'

wood

pump.

An' when you had to prime it, then they was an awful fuss;
The girls 'ud git the wotter pails and make a dredful muss,
Spillin' more outside'n in; you could hyur it splashin' down,
Dashin' round aginst milk things 'ith a holler, far off soun';
Perty quick the pump 'ud sniffle; then he'd sorter turn an' growl;
Then, ez if he didn't like it, he 'ud jes' git up an' howl;
An' before you hardly know'd it 'ud hyur a little thump,
An' the wotter 'ud be flowin' from

the ol'

wood

pump.

(University Review, University of Kansas, X, June 1889, 273; *Collection of Kansas Poetry,* Hattie Horner, compiler, 1891.)

High Five on Willow Creek

Sissiety in Willerville 'us always kinder slow,
We bein' all homebodies like, an' not much on the go;
A course we had our soshebuls and spellin' schools and sich,
An' played crokay an' checkers but we never seemed to itch
Fer highfallutin' games of chance like poker, drew er whist,
That bein' 'genst the principuls of every Methodist,
But all our former piety 'at usta bloom and thrive,
Is busted into smithereens by this High Five.

We olders strove agenst it with our prayers night an' day,
An' ast the Lord to he'p us drive the wily imp away;
But Providence had willed it so it wasn't any use;
An' so the game jes' took the town, like Satan running loose.
An' sir, before we knowed it our own girls 'us playin' too,
An' I jes' kinder pickt it up, you know like people do;
It's somethin' like ol' sledge, you see, the best ol' game alive,
An' so I took a likin' to this new High Five.

The girls they got to goin' out more'n they'd ever done,
A bringin' home ther soovyneers an' prizes 'at they'd won.
 An' onct when they got home one night, perhaps a leetle late,
They ketched their paw and maw undressed, an' warmin' by the grate.
It must a plagued ther fellows some, although we lit right out;
An' so to make things even just ez sure as you're alive,
We let the girls have company at home to play High Five.

They low'd they must get up the folks a cold bite er a snack,
A lunch I guess they called it an' as we just had a stack
Of peach perserves, apple jell, and picklelilly too,
I hinted 'at they use 'em but law me that wouldn't do;
They went an' had a checken killed an' made up into hash,
An' bought a lot of oysters an' a peck of other trash;

* * * * * * * * * *

So when I come to pay for it ez near's I can arrive,
I think the game should be High Ten instid of called High Five.

(El Dorado Republican, January 10, 1890; *The Lance,* June 14, 1890; *Current Literature,* Vol.10, 152. "High Five" was a four-player card game, more elaborate than Auction Pitch, where the trump suit included the five of the other suit of the same color.)

Literchoor on Willer Crick

Down on Willer Crick they isn't
    Very much a what you'd call
Literary spirit; 'tisn't
    In the atmosphere atall;
Lots more ager[1] an' malarey[2]
    Circulatin' 'n the breeze,
Then they is a literary
    Inspiration er idees
They's just on'y one exception —
    Come to git right down't the rub,
That's the crowd 'at bears the caption
    Of "The Ash Pile Club."

Meets whever is most handy,
    At the court house er town pump:
Fer refreshment peanut candy
    Seems to strike the spot 'bout plump.
Byron,[3] Shakespeare,[4] Ella Wheeler,[5]
    Carleton,[6] Saxe,[7] and Moore,[8]
Bellamy[9] and Miss Ameeler
    Rives[10] an' three er four
Furrin' fellers, like ol' Moosyer
    Zola[11] they kin cote;
An' Jim Riley,[12] thet air Hoosier —
    Know him off by rote.

Other ev'nin' got to gasin'
    'Bout what was the smoothes' piece
Ever writ; a feller passin'
    Said "Don Wan"[13] was slick as grease:
Jedge 'lowed "Little Nell"[14] was sweeter;
    Others held for "Lally Rook:"[15]
Som'un said "Luceel"[16] was neater
    'An the things in airy book.
Then sez I "As we're a seekin'

Meaty, intyleckshul grub —
Pork has tender-lines wuth speakin'
Of before the Ash Pile Club."

(*El Dorado Republican,* February 7, 1890; *Current Literature,* Vol. 10, 152. • 1.
Ague; malarial fever. • 2. Malaria • 3. Byron, George Gordon Byron, Baron (1788-
1824). • 4. William Shakespeare (1564-1616). • 5. Ella Wheeler Wilcox (1850-1919).
• 6. Will Carleton (1845-1912). • 7. Hermann Maurice Saxe (1696-1750). • 8. Tho-
mas Moore (1779-1852). • 9. Edward Bellamy (1850-1898). • 10. Amelie Rives
(1863-1945), also known as: Princess Troubetzkoy; Amelie Rives-Chandler; and
Amelie Rives Troubetzkoy. • 11. Monsieur Emil Zola (1840-1902). • 12. James
Whitcomb Riley (1849-1916). • 13. "Don Juan," poem by George Gordon Byron. •
14. "Little Nell," poem by Charles John Huffam Dickens (1812-1870). • 15. "Lalla
Rookh," poem by Thomas Moore. • 16. "Lucile," poem by Owen Meredith, pseud-
onym of Edward Robert Bulwer Lytton, 1st Earl of Lytton, British statesman and
poet 1831-1891).

———

The Meetin' House Steps

Somehow ruther Willerville is kinder changed to me —
Not sayin' 'taint a bigger town an' all it orto be —
But leastways with those fixin's on, I can't jes git things straight.
I miss the good ol' land marks 'at I knew in semty-eight.
Where is the ol' stone school house; an' where's the ol' town pump?
Where has the *hotel* gone to an' what's come a ol' Jedge Bump?
The on'y thing 'at's round here now 'at 'pears to stir the dep's
Of bygone recollections is the

the meetin'

house

steps.

I mind how all us younguns useto hang around there nights;
It was the baste[1] fer hid' an' seek an' where we had ar fights,
An' when we got through playin' "ricollec"[2] how Chink an' Bud
'Ud tell us big ghost stories 'at 'ud fairly freeze ar blood.

An' so when we got bigger, it was nacher'l we should go
Of ev'nin's to the ol' steps to have ar talk you know.
We'd talk of how when we growed up we'd do great things, perhaps
— But boy dreams got no furder'n
                                        the meetin'
                                                house
                                                        steps.

Another reason why I like the ol' steps donchew see; —
We use' to count the stars there summer ev'nin's her an' me.
I somehow got a notion 'at the beauty of a thing
Ain't in its form an' color, but in memories 'at cling
'An cluster all around it; now ferrinstance take the moon —
A old an' faded gord — yit purty as a tune
'At's strained thro' mixed-up fancies of a dream, because it heps
To bring me back 'ith Idy on
                                        the meetin'
                                                house
                                                        steps.

So if the steps is standin' after I have passed away —
When the choir has got done singin' an' the parson's had his say,
An' when the folks 'at want to look has passed around the aisle,
I wisht 'at they 'u'd take me out to rest a little while;
Jes' lay me down there quiet like, stretched out an' peerin' thro'
The fleecy clouds of heaven, es I use' to like to do
Of shady summer afternoons, and if the Lord accep's
This soul at all, He'll do it from
                                        the meetin'
                                                house
                                                        steps.

(El Dorado Republican, March 7, 1890. • 1. Baste, i.e., base. • 2. ricollec, i.e., the game of telling tall tales.)

Black Bass Fishing

A sparkling stream
Where pebbles gleam
Broad spreading elms
The banks o'er hanging.
A soft south wind,
A quiet friend,
A boat and rod,
A graceful "chub"
To tempt them
From their hiding.
   A cast, a gleam,
   A swirling foam,
   A fight for life;
But alas, too soon,
Ere scarce begun
The victory's won.
The sun goes down,
The day is done:
Nay, not done
While summer's biding.

(El Dorado Republican, May 23, 1890; December 18, 1891. The black bass is part of a group that includes largemouth, smallmouth and spotted basses. Common in farm ponds, lakes and slow-moving streams around El Dorado, they usually associate with cover such as aquatic vegetation or submerged timber.)

A Memory of Willer Crick

In the gawky, gangling girlhood of the spring, and ere the lass
Has rosy lips and sky-blue eyes or dimples of the grass;
The ground is soft and soggy in the timber, and the birds
Sing o-be-joyful love songs and their anthems without words.
The telegraph wires hum the bass, and, clearing of her throat,
The old crick at the ford croons in her low contralto note,
Tar up the old flat-bottomed boat and make her water-tight,
For soon the day is coming when the bass begin to bite.

(Kansas City Journal, February 28, 1892)

———

A Breath from Willer Crick

Lew[1], do you remember old Willer Crick mill,
    On Uncle Abe Hoskinson's place,
Where we used to go ev'ry Sunday until
    Folks said 'twas a public disgrace?
The girls used to put up fried chicken and bread,
    And pickles and cake filled with figs;
While we used to hitch up old Tommy and Ted
    To one of those two-seated rigs.
We used to ride home through the cool summer night —
    I'd manage to drive going down —
But, Lew, do you mind how I claimed as my right
    The back seat a-coming to town?

We didn't have chaperones then, bless your soul —
    Too early for them, I believe —
And so we were honest, I think on the whole,
    We'd no one along to deceive.

I knew you were "gone," though you never would say —
    You guessed the same thing from my tone —
The girls likely soon saw just how the ground lay,
    And talked it all over alone.
But, my! weren't we proper and prim going out,
When day wore his radiant crown —
But somehow a strange and weird change came about
    On the back seat a-coming to town.

Remember the fellows on Rackensack bend
    Who used to give "bids" to their "rags?"
We always invited the girls to attend,
    And hired two of Peterson's nags.
Bill Jones would call off in his own wooly way,
    "Sif Sand Sal" and "Hogs in the corn."
Injoining the guests on the floor to "chaw hay"
    Till nearly the gray hour of morn.
Of course, we were played out, but none ever sighed,
    Nor did any brow ever frown,
For each had a hope that perhaps he might ride
    On the back seat a-coming to town.

Old man, we have wandered some, hither and yon,
    Since we lived and loved on the crick:
We've seen maidens comely and fair to look on,
    And turn-outs² that made ours look sick.
But tell me what magic has gilded those days
    To make them look brighter than these?
What old-fashioned fairy has turned into haze,
    The clouds that low'red over those leas?
Of course we are happier now than we were,
    And have fewer sorrows to drown —
But I'd give to-day up, for one sip from the cup,
    On the back seat a-coming to town.

(*Kansas City Journal*, July 18, 1892. • 1. Probably Lew Schmucker, White's child-hood friend, later hired by White as bookkeeper, news reporter and ad salesman for the *Gazette*. • 2. Turned out in fine clothes.)

Willer Crick in June

Up here in the city it's just hot and hot and hot;
They haint no use in huntin' for a comf'tabular spot
Than that which you are fryin' in: the pavement and the sun
Can double teams and smother you and if you try to run
Or sneak or circumvent 'em — use your fan or umberell
You set your blood to streamin' till it almost seems to jell.
O the city is the city always hot and out of tune
With a man who thinks of Willer Crick — say long about in June.

For I'm just a yearnin', and a yearnin' to be there,
And set in front of Gordon's, tiled in a Wabbly chair,
A holdin' out my shirt sleeves for the breeze to trickle down
My wrist and round my collar like it won't do here in town.
I want to feel the coolness that the sprinkler wagon brings;
I want to be in swimmin' with the harvest crew— 'y jings —
And have 'em take the horses in. Hey? By the great horn spoon
Just splosh and whoop in Willer Crick — say long about in June.

I wouldn't mind to set a hour awaitin' for the train
Say on the northeast corner of the depot — me and Crane —
A gassin' 'bout who's married who, and who we used to guess
Would make it, and a speculatin' on their happiness.
And feelin' chunks of comfort oozin' through you with the breeze
And steppin' so high mentally that skittish book idees
Come up and feed out of your hand like when you see the moon
And think about your sweethearts — well, that's Willer Crick in June.

But up here in the city it's just hot and hot and hot
And every place you go is worse than airy other spot
You've been to yet, and everywheres the pavement and the sun
They go cahoots to cook you and to boil you good and done.
O our fan it stirs the kettle and as for your umberell
It only claps the cover on and lets you steam and swell.
O the city is the city and it's always out of tune
With a man who thinks of Willer Crick — say long about in June.

(Kansas City Star, July 1, 1894)

13

POLITICS

THE VOTING PRECINCTS.

Politics on Willer Creek

Things is what you'd call onsettled, down on Mud an' Willer Cricks;
Farmers kind o' feelun nettled, bout a run a politics
Organized a sub-alliance, number semty-two;
Bid the world an' flesh defiance, a,' the devil too.
        An' I tell you
                They're go'n' to do
                        Somepin tull surprise a few.

Histed up a county ticket, mostly Dimycrats an' sich:
Some folks think 'at they can lick it, cause Liance[1] men won't hitch.
Howsomeever it'll hustle, any one-hoss candidate,
To do up thet tower of muscle: Kernal Hucks[2] or Upper Slate.
        Lemme see:
                Seems to me
                        Bill[3] kim here in semty-three.

Bill has always ben a figger: first he run for congers; then'
Run fer Jedge an' found it bigger 'en he was: so fin'ly when
Hucks see comin' from Iowey didn't make him any votes,
He put up his drippun bowie,[4] an' went in to raisun shoats.[5]
        He'd come to town
                And hang aroun'
                        An' howl 'bout things a runnun down.

When he found 'at plain stock raisun didn't seem to fill his jeans,
Bill begun, with grace amazun, ped'lin' organs an' machines:
Doctored hosses: took to teachun: an' 'long there in semty-eight,
Dern ef Kernel wa'n't a preachun 'round up near the head of State.
        He'd keep his lick
                Up an' jes' kick
                        'Till folks us purty blame near sick.

Still he hung onto his quarter,[6] on the muddy Upper State,
So he felt as if he'd 'orter be a farmer's candidate.
Never knowed to work a lick, he come to town bout every day;

Ast him how's things up the crick he jes' would sober up an' say:
  "Purty bad"
      'N'en he'd add:
          "What kind times 'a you folks had?"

Beun up in social science, Kernel struck his gate,
Gittun in the sub-alliance, on the Upper Slate.
When they put him on the ticket, y'orter hyurd his speech:
Wa'n't a thing he didn't kick, 'at come within his reach.
      But *thet air* kick
          Will look blame sick
              When he reads the returns from Willer Crick.

(El Dorado Republican, June 20, 1890; *The Lance* (Topeka), June 21, 1890. • 1. Farmers' Alliance. • 2. and 3. Colonel William "Bill" Hucks of the Upper Slate creek near Hamilton in Greenwood County, Kansas was elected as a delegate to the State Republican League convention in Topeka. • 4. A large, straight, single-edged hunting knife. • 5. Young hogs. • 6. A quarter acre.)

———

In Districk Forty-Two

He lives in Centre township, Uncle Billie Sturges does,
Cross the crick from Silas Johnson, where Bird City usto was;
He built the Sturges school house, an' I want to say to you,
He was the leadin' farmer out in Districk 42.

He runs the literary an' he speaks when folks debate:
Resolved, 'at fire heats water er is jest about ez great;
He's way up in religion, and at prayin' they is few
Kin beat ol' Billie Sturges out in Districk 42.

There never was a meetin' savorin' of politics,
'At he haint bin a war hoss in sence eighteen sempty-six.
An' ef you want to get there, now I tell you what you do:
See Uncle Billie Sturges out in Districk 42.

He's kinder got the run a things and sorter knows the boys,
From Huckes, up in Blaine township, to Sims, in Illinoys,
An' he kin steer you 'mongst 'em better'n anyone kin do,
Kin Uncle Billie Sturges out in Districk 42.

He comes to town a month before election day,
An' loafs around an' gasses in a very knowin' way;
But ast what he thinks ol' Centre township's go'n' to do,
He'll say: "They vote 'ith Sturges out in Districk 42."

So when this 'ere alliance[1] move kim floatin' out our way;
What should ol' Billie Sturges do, but catch on, ez they say;
He hooped it up to Shylock an' the corporations too,
An' took the hull thing with him out in Districk 42.

He sees how things was goin', though, when we begin to mix
In that air smokin' cauldron designated politics,
So tryin' hard to wiggle out an' findin' 'twouldn't do,
Sezee: "Less vote'r straight, for luck, in Districk 42."

But when he rid to town an' see the way the thing kim out —
Hyurd the other fellows yellin', when he hyurd the Demmies shout —
Sezee to them air Demmies: "No you're goldarn smart ain't you,
Next year you'll see a difference out in Districk 42."

(El Dorado Republican, November 14, 1890. • 1. The Farmers' Alliance, organized
in Kansas in 1890.)

———

Alas, Poor Yorick!

Heroes come and heroes go;
        Laurels fade and wither:
Like the leaves wild winds blow,
        Swirling here and thither.
Are the names of fate tossed up
        Now on high a minute,
Then gently sink
        To Lethe's[1] brink,
And lo! they are not in it.

Today the world is smiling on
        A little baby face;
Today the world is piling on
        Its tribute to her grace:
Today one sits without a song
        And hears another win it.
The Cleveland kid[2]
        Has got the bid,
And young McKee's[3] not in it.

But yesterday the world stood still
        And potentates were quiet.
While young McKee had got his fill
        Of romp and baby riot;
But yesterday a case of cramps —
        And nations stopped to thin it,
And yet today
        The people say
That young McKee's not in it.

(El Dorado Republican, October 2, 1891. • 1. In Greek mythology, this river in Hades caused forgetfulness of the past when its water was drunk. • 2. Stephen Grover Cleveland (1837-1908) was 22nd and 24th President of the U.S., having been reelected to the presidency over Benjamin Harrison in 1892. • 3. This was likely Leonard V. McKee (1845-1916), a Civil War veteran from Ohio who moved to Frankfort, Kansas, where he became a banker. See also the *Handbook of the Kansas Legislature, 1901,* Topeka, Kansas, 1900.

A Tribute to "Jackson"

There are those who sing of royal bouts in tournament and court;
There are those who sing of noble deeds and knightly games and sport;
And those who sing of chivalry and those who sing the praise
Of good old times in ancient rhymes and good old-fashioned lays;
But other times aren't in it and other fete days pall
Before the Priest of Pallas[1] day and Colonel "Jackson's" ball.[2]

The corn-fed Kansas beauties and paw-paw[3] belles are there,
And mingle in the mazy[4] with jet beads set in their hair;
The youth of wealth and fashion from Jasper County whirls
In a mad'ning dizzy day dream with the Jackson County girls;
While the silver musts[5] of music on the raptured senses fall,
At the fete of Priests of Pallas thro' the night of "Jackson's" ball.

The lady-like young gentleman[6] with his low-cut fancy vest,
And his sweet-faced, coy typewriter girl are present in their best.
The pride and joy of Wabash and of Troost and of Belleview
Vie in the race for elegance with Union Avenue.
And all this blaze of glory, this tinseled pageant all
Is at the Priests of Pallas show at Colonel Jackson's" ball.

Perhaps there is a heaven where an angel choir sings,
Perhaps there is a joyous day which follows earthly things;
Perhaps the bliss we look for will send ecstatic thrills
Thro' the soul of every living mote and shake the gray old hills —
But say, if this arrangement for the future works out at all,
It will pattern after Pallas and the Colonel "Jackson's" ball.

(*Kansas City Journal,* October 8, 1891. • 1. The Priests of Pallas festivals were annual attractions in Kansas City, Missouri, between 1887 through 1924. Pallas was, in Greek mythology, a giant slain by Athena in the war between the Olympians and the giants. • 2. "Colonel Jackson" was an anonymous name ascribed to the mysterious person who compiled and sent hundreds of invitations to those eligible to attend "Jackson's Ball." After the "Ball List" had been sent, not even the High Priests of Pallas could secure another of the prized invitations. • 3. The oblong, yellowish fruit of the paw-paw tree. • 4. Perplexed, as if with turns or windings of a maze. • 5. A silver hair powder. • 6. The "Queens" of the Priests of Pallas festivals were disguised men, and their identities were never revealed during these festival events. It was felt that the parade and other activities were too strenuous for women.)

Simpson Slumped

There is woe and desolation in the land beyond the Kaw;[1]
There is grief and desperation far across the Arkansas;[2]
Come the sad and tearful tidings from the plutocratic East
That the new fledged Sunflower[3] statesman joined a Democratic feast;
>   And that Jerry[4]
>   Ordered Sherry
>   And was erstwhile gay and merry,
While the "poor oppressed" were very
>   Much fatigued to say the least.

A year ago the welkin[5] rang with Jerry's tale of woe
And the crooning Kansas cyclone was not in it with his blow,
As he waded into Wall Street or attacked the railroad grants,
But today his star has dropped afar and Jerry's name is trousers,
>   And therefore
>   They are sore —
>   And the yeoman[6] and what's more,
Jerry may come back as marshal in the good old days of yore
>   Now perchance.

What will then become of Shylock?[7] Who will crush the money power?
Who will "educate the masses" on the questions of the hour?
Who will fix the wealth "per capita" and who will throw the lance
That will "stab the robber tariff?" Who will regulate finance?
>   Who will know
>   How to show
>   Providence the way things go?
In this chorus of calamity, this nightmare maze of woe,
>   Who'll lead the dance?

(Kansas City Journal, October 14, 1891; *El Dorado Republican,* October 23, 1891, title was "Simpson Stumped. • 1.-2. Rivers in Kansas. • 3. The Kansas State flower. • 4. Jeremiah "Sockless Jerry" Simpson (1842-1905), Populist congressman from Medicine Lodge, Kansas. • 5. The air or sky. • 6. An attendant who performed menial services. • 7. An extortionate creditor.)*

Not for a Minute

The scrub oak and the willow have been painted gaudy red,
    By the daring free hand pencil of the Frost;
The prairie grass is dusty, and the summer plants are dead,
    And their tender verdant splendor all is lost.
This, of course, does not refer to our police commission
    Nor the order that we take our Sundays dry;
        As they drank a little drinklet,
        As they thank a large-sized thinklet
        Oh, they wank a knowing winklet
            In the corner of their eye.

They'll fry the fat from all the joints on Union Avenue,
    From Walnut Street and Delaware to Troost;
And tell the bar-keep to come down with boodle[1] in the view
    Of having funds to give their men a boost.
But, of course, it's not for closing that the order has been made,
    Unless the boys don't put up when they call.
        With their fingers to their noses
        Where there linger hectic roses
        Is there any one supposes
            That they want 'em closed at all?

(Kansas City Journal, October 22, 1891. Kansas City's ward and precinct boundaries
were shown on maps in the *Kansas City Star* on November 7, 1892, February 19,
1894 and April 2, 1894. • 1. Bribe money.)

The Return of Jim

Have you noticed that there's something circulating in the air
That is bracing and displacing all the microbes of despair?
Have you noticed in the trade reports so lately very slow,
That the figure now is bigger than it was a month ago ?
Have you noticed that the stars and stripes the autumn breezes crack
Somewhat louder and much prouder
Now that Jim's got back?

Have you noticed out in Kansas how the boys are falling in?
How the growlers' and the howlers' ranks are growing very thin?
Have you noticed how the Kansas porkers proudly curl their tails,
As though to try to give the lie to demagogic wails?
Have you noticed how the wheat and corn and fodder in the stack
Are what you term extremely firm
Since Jim's got back?

Have you noticed down in Chile that they're lying very low;
That his skinny nibs Rudini plays is pianissimo?
Have you seen the brown plush muffle[1] on the British lion's roar?
Though soft as seal, it is not seal,[2] and hides an ugly sore,
But you'll notice that your Uncle Sam's not taking any slack
From any one-horse power throne
Since Jim's got back.

Republicans and Democrats rejoice to see old Jim;
He has a way, you can't gainsay; we are all proud of him.
The Massachusetts Yankee and the planter "down Mobile"
In old Jim Blaine[3] are joined again a royal glory feel
In living in a nation that can give the world a whack;
For Uncle Sam won't care a cent
Since Jim's got back.

(*Kansas City Journal,* October 29, 1891. • 1. To wrap with something to deaden the sound. • 2. Seal's fur. • 3. James Gillespie Blaine (1830-1893), American diplomat, influential in Pan-American movement.)

The Facts as to Mr. Gilluley

Wud yez shquint at that fly copper, goun shtruttin' down the shtreet,
Jist git onto thim elasthics that're fastened to his feet.
Howly mither! What a check-rein:[1] watch 'im give the byes the shnub,
Wud yez nothice how he shwings hisself, and how he shakes his club?
You wud know he was a new man by his shiney togs, av coorse,
Oh, Gilluley, av the sivinth ward, is just come on the force.

Missus Martin sez he pays hor for the apples that he takes;
And the cuke at Major Slaytor's trows away hor buckwheat cakes;
He's reported Denny Collins, Jamsey Doane and Fatty Hawes,
For a kapun opun side doors, as fornist the Sunday laws;
Whin he towld ut up at Cintril, Sargint laft till he was hooarse,
For Gilluley, av the Sivinth ward, is jist come on the foorce.

He's respectful and politeful to the leddies on the square;
And he tells the joys from Atchinson where all the Turners are,
Which is loike thim siction Dirish, so obsequious and gay —
Why, he actchually stands aside and gives the Dootch half way;
And to hear 'im answer questions fills the owld wid remoorse —
For Gilluley, av the Sivinth ward, is jist come on the force.

(Kansas City Journal, January 5, 1892. • 1. A short rein looped over a hook on the
saddle of a harness to prevent a horse from lowering its head.)

A Paving Pastoral

Say: All de fellies on de row[1] has struck a dead new game;
Youse don' git pinched fer playun, and de swag is just de same;
Youse hit de mark dot runs de ward, an' tells him dat you be
A guy dat don' know how to vote; he fixes you out. See?
Youse go an' do de votin' where he says, an' takes de tin;[2]
An' hell will be a poppin' when de gang gits in.

De heavy swell[3] out dere on Troost', de nibs[4] dat lives on Oak —
We's go'n to pipe fer boodle,[5] an' we'll never skip a bloke.
Say: Dis pollin' game is dead sure safe, an' more'n dat — it's new;
It beats ol' seven-leven[6] gettin' action on yer glue.[7]
De gang is go'n to play it, and de gang it always win,
An it's hell will be a poppin' when de gang gits in.

Look yonder at dat mean ol' mug go wingin' up de walk;
Dat's Bill; he's got a chisel gall;[8] youse otter hear his talk,
He sez de town is rotten an' de game is on the drag;
It's beautiful to stand around when Ol' Bill chews de rag;
Dem high rollers dey don' like it; but deir talk don' go; it's thin —
Fer hell will be a poppin' when de gang gits in.

(Kansas City Journal, February 23, 1892. • 1. This was "Battle Row"; see also "The Returns on 'de Row.' " • 2. Money. • 3.-4. Dandies on Troost and Oak Streets. • 5. Bribe money. • 6. Crap shooting. • 7. Any gambling objective. • 8. A cheating, irritating behavior.)

A Ballad of the Small Property Owner

In old days the robbers lived out in the woods
    Or dwelt in a hole in the ground,
And cheerfully froze to the traveler's goods
    Whenever he happened around.
Oh, the robber of old
    Was simple and bold,
And rarely put on any frills;
    But the robber today
        Has a quite different way,
           And the taxpayers foot up the bills —
Bills — bills — the taxpayers settle the bills.

The old-fashioned robber was deft with his dirk,[1]
    The robber today wears a smile;
With a murderous club No. 1 did his work,
    No. 2 uses "grease"[2] from his "pile!"[3]
The olden time gang
    Often festively sang
While doling its death dealing pills;[4]
    Its latter day friend
        Blandly moves to amend —
           And the taxpayers look after the bills —
Bills — bills — the taxpayers settle the bills.

The Queen Anne highwayman was meek as a lamb
    When the law called on him to atone;
The paving contractor does not care — anything hardly,
    But rigs up a law of his own.
Oh, the brave Robin Hood,
    Who was moderately good,
Never lugged off the eternal hills;[5]
    But his heir at law trots
        Off with houses and lots,
           And the taxpayers sigh at the bills —
Bills — bills — the taxpayers settle the bills.

(Kansas City Journal, February 24, 1892. Each property owner was to be assessed for road-paving along his property line next to the road, but opponents insisted that Kansas City should be responsible for paving costs. • 1. A dagger. • 2.-3. To offer bribes from his fortune. • 4. Poisons. • 5. Robin Hood never robbed excessively large quantities of loot.)

Paving with Gold

In the old-fashioned church that stood on the hill,
    Just back from the old-fashioned road,
The parson of old-fashioned days used to fill
His old-fashioned sermons with heaven and thrill
His old-fashioned flock with its splendor, until
    They longed for their future abode.
They believed every word of the story he told:
Of the beautiful city with streets paved with gold.

The old-fashioned building still stands on the height;
    Around it a city has grown:
A few of the flock have taken their flight
Above to the golden-paved city of light;
The others who stay here and pay taxes might
(If the gang didn't steal so and manage things right)
    Have golden-paved streets of their own.
If all of the boodling[1] and swindles were told,
The town could be paved with eighteen-karat gold.

(Kansas City Journal, February 25, 1892. • 1. Bribing, graft).

————

The "Small Property Owner"

Sez 'e: "Gud marnin', Dinny," and sez Oi, "Gud marnin', sor;"
Sez 'e: Oi hope yer feelin' well." Oi sed I t'ot Oi wor.
Sez 'e: "How air yez go'n to vote?" so tinder loike an kind.
"Wid paper ballots," Oi sez Oi to aise his achin' mind.
"How 'bout thim ere amindmints?" sed 'e, showin' of his hand.
Sez Oi: "Oi am ferninst 'em," still remainin' shweet and bland.
"We'll make the rich min foot the bills, and sthick ut to 'em hard,"
Sez 'e, "an' give the poor man work upon the boolyvard."
    Yez kin fuddle Patsey Hoolahan an' Grohan and McTurk,
    Wid yer blarney 'bout the poor man an' yer promises av work —
    But yez can't fool Dinny Collins by a damsite.

"How air yez go'n to sthick the rich?" sez Oi to him, sez Oi,
"By dumpin' taxes on the lots," sez 'e, a winkin' sly.
"Phwat lots?" sez Oi. "The rich min's lots," sez 'e to me, sez 'e.
"They're paved already," Oi sez Oi. "Go out yourself an' see."
"They's them that ain't paved, though," 'e sez. "Av coorse," sez Oi, "but thin
Thim lots is on the shtreets where live the hard-up workin' min."
We won't touch thim," sez 'e. "You won't?" Thin aimin' fer his eyes:
"Phwere is the work a comin' from yez promised to the byes?"
> Yez kin' fuddle Patsey Hoolahan, an' Groghan an' McTurk,
> Wid yer blarney 'bout the poor man an' yer promises av work —
> But yes can't fool Dinny Collins by a damsite.

"We'll give ut to 'em some way," sez 'e, holdin' up his end.
"An' add ut to the taxes that we're payin' now, me friend."
Sez 'e: "Yer work upon the sthreets will pay yer tax an' more."
"Oi'm only one, an' ut will drive tin thousand from our door;
Tin thousand min who want to come wid stiddy work for all
Will go around; they cannot climb that boodle[1] pavin' wall."
"We'll beat yez anyhow," sez 'e, "an' put the whole thing through."
"The workin' min will pay the bribes yez give 'em if ye do.
> Yez kin fuddle Patsey Hoolahan an' Groghan an' McTurk
> Wid yer blarney 'bout the poor man, an' yer promises av work,
> But yez can't fool Dinny Collins by a damsite.

Sez 'e: "Gud marnin', Dinny," and sez Oi, "Gud marnin', sor;"
Sez 'e: "Oi hope yer feelin' well." Oi said Oi t'ot Oi wor.
But as Oi saw him prance the sthreets a puttin' up the drinks,
"Who's payin' thot man's wages and his liquor bills?" Oi thinks.
The lab'rin' min ain't doin' ut, who're workin' by the day;
An' yit he's workin' for thim same, if yez believe his say,
Who drives on this darn pavin' wid ther four in hands[2] and sich?
Who pays the loikes av him fer work? The poor man or the rich?
> Yez can fuddle Patsey Hoolahan, an' Grighan, and McTurk
> Wid yer blarney 'bout the poor man an' yer promises av work —
> But yez can't fool Dinny Collins by a damsite.

(*Kansas City Journal,* February 26, 1892. • 1. Bribe money or graft. • 2. Four horses arranged in two teams driven tandem by one person. Another simile designates a kind of necktie tied with a slip-knot. Both meanings imply a dangerous traffic mixture on the paved streets.)

And I Vote "YES"

We live out here on Washington, ma an' the girls an' me:
The girls go in society, such as they is, you see —
We live in that brick mansion where them portoricoes[1] are —
It's stylisher than any in the neighborhood by far;
While of course it hain't so tony[2] as we used to have back East,
It's good enough fer pore folks an' 'tull do, to say the least;
A course, we has this pavin', as you call it, but I can guess
That bein' as the others hain't, why I'll vote "yes."

Say, have you saw our bran new hack?[3] You hain't? Well, I declare!
You probably didn't reco'nize them coats of arms we wear;
Law me! Yes, they're spick span new, an' strickly up to date;
An' that black nigger driver is especially oh fate.[4]
When we ride on the bullyvard, an' turn the top down, My!
You orto see 'em stare at us as we go prancin' by.
But that's a gittin' common, an' we can't go ut unless
They lay down some new pavin'; an' so I vote "yes."

I got some outside property endurin' of the boom[5]
Out in the edge of Westport where they've lots of breathin' room;
Ma an' me was talking of the thing the other day
An' ma she said she thought that it was kinder this a way;
Westport lots is healthful an' is well drained an' all that,
But they will never raise until they're easier got at
An' if the streets that lead out there was paved, why then I guess
We'd have no trouble sellin', an' so I vote "yes."

These folks who talk of taxes an' economy as well;
They irritate we upper ten,[6] beyond the power to tell.
Our streets are paved all right enough; we paved 'em long ago,
When we was makin' money; an' why can't them folks do so?
We've formed a pavin' company, in our exclusive set;
We're a go'ne to make some ducats[7] if the thing goes through, you bet.
The girls is goin' out this spring; each one will want a dress;
I'll need some dough to pay fer 'em, so I'll vote "Yes."

(Kansas City Journal, February 27, 1892. All the proposed charter amendments were
carried at the special election, but resulted in a small vote. Out of a total registration
of about 39,000, only about 8,500 voted. • 1. Porticoes were colonnades or covered

walkways to houses. • 2. Colloquial for stylish, well-kept. • 3. A rented, horse-drawn carriage or coach. • 4. Au fait: an expert, or one familiar with the facts. • 5. The economic upturn of the 1880s. • 6. The upper ten percent of society. • 7. A gold coin of several European countries.)

A True Bill[1]

In the ball room, where the perfume of the lilies and the rose
Mingles with the liquid languors of the pleading waltz that blows
Petulantly like the east wind rustling in the trees of June,
Like turning back of lovers' sighs breathed to'ard the rising moon —
In the splendor of the ball room, in the scene of giddy grace,
Where chandeliers pour softened lights upon his shell-pink face:
Where woman's silver laughter chains the god of pleasure near —
There he is the chiefest idol — there they call him "Wullie, dear."

On the glaring, flaring posters, in the large, fierce-looking type,
Proudly hung upon the dead wall, lording o'er the guttersnipe:
In the mouths of modest matrons, and of portly, pompous sires,
On the lips of would-be schemers — men who think they pull the wires;
In the ears of pious strangers, who are learning all they can
Of the youth, the fixers whisper: "He's a 'very nice young man.' "
And to clinch the sweet assertion, and to keep opponents still,
It is printed, spoken, written, peddled through the town as "Will."[2]

In de 'Ate' ward it is different, and down in de Nint' ward, see?
Dem ere marks dey's heard from Andy[3] who dere man's a-go'n' to be;
Say, dat goes, dat talk of Andy's. Andy knows dis here young bloke;
Andy says dat he's sure in it, youse jes' watch ol' Andy's smoke;
All dem guys up town support him, all dem dead straight people, too —
What's de dif, de gang dey owns him; what dem fly marks go'n' to do?
Yes, we's heard dey slobber on him, and de Star[4] it calls him "Will";
Dat's a bluff, fer dem dat owns him — all us fellies calls him "Bill."

(Kansas City Journal, March 23, 1892. • 1. "Bill" of the "Ate" ward was William A. Skinner, a good businessman who made a fine impression on Kansas City's eighth ward Republican voters for the city election on April 5, 1892. Skinner was candidate for eighth-ward member of the Lower House, but lost the election. • 2. White here uses the name "Will" to represent William S. Cowherd, candidate for Democratic mayor of Kansas City, and was head of the Democratic city ticket that was supported by thieves, thugs, barrel-house bums and runners for disreputable houses. He later won the election. • 3. Andrew P. Foley was one of Kansas City's Democratic combine bosses and candidate for the second ward member of the Lower House. He also won his election. • 4. *Kansas City Star.)*

A Free Salt River Trip

I'm a congressman, alas,
And I've come to such a pass,
As I've recently through private sources learned,
That, though toiling hard and late,
For my country and my state,
It is possible I may not be returned.

At the races I have been
Always prompt, and tried to win,
Though I've oftentimes bet on the losing nag;
At the ball games I have done
Somewhat better — there I've won
Quite a decent little pocketful of swag.

Yet amazing to relate,
My own district — base ingrate! —
Does not credit me with brilliant statesmanship;
It's preparing, so I hear
In this president year,
To present me with a free Salt River trip.

(Kansas City Journal, May (i.e., April) 22, 1892. White initialed his article entitled, "The Kansas Conflict" which included this poem. See also his poem, "And Now in Conclusion," note number 2.)

———

(Untitled)

His form was bent, his step was slow;
His piping voice was weak,
The fire of youth had ceased to glow
Upon his pallid cheek.

He peered into the jostling throng,
　　But held himself apart,
As though he felt some cruel wrong,
　　Gnaw at his mildewed heart.

"Whence comest thou, — my good man gray,"
　　Up spake a lusty youth.
Each voice was stilled that he might say:
　　He gave no heed, forsooth.

"Whence goest thou, grim sire, most kind?"
　　Quoth one from Bitter Creek;
And as they hushed they heard the wind
　　Through his chinchilla's leak.[1]

He spake nor made a mortal sound,
　　But reached beneath his coat.
And there a well-worn parchment found —
　　On it these words he wrote:

"I prithee, prithee, leave me here,
　　In this, my lonely walk.
I'm oiling up my thinking gear —
　　'Tis not my time to talk."

"I'm vainly thinking all the day
　　From dawn to setting sun:
'Where is the man who used to say —
　　What has old Ingalls done?' "

(Kansas City Journal, May 19, 1892; Republican senator John James Ingalls (1833-1900) of Kansas was defeated by a Democratic-Populist ("Demo-Pop") machine in 1892. • 1. Ingalls often wore a long overcoat with a fur collar — hence, the allusion to a rodent's "leak," or hole, which lets wastes escape.)

The Ballade of the Nameless Knight

Upon the king's main traveled road,
    With gaudy banner floating high;
An errant knight in armor bright,
    Sallied on a prancing palfrey by.
Upon his banner there was writ
    No sign to tell his king or cause,
Nor did there slip from out his lip
    A syllable of who he was.
The gateman let the 'cullis[1] fall:
    "I charge thee, nameless warrior, stop."
He whispered low: "Pray let me go,
    I am a Demo-pop."[2]

Up spake the doughty gateman then
    "Thou wear'st no color on thy spear;
In whose defence wouldst thou go hence;
    Plunk down thy royal passport here."
The knight stood still; a knowing smile
    Curled on the cunning gateman's lip:
"If you have nerve you may observe
    Upon my shoulder this here chip."
He dared not call the gateman's bluff,
    This knight who let his cutlass drop,
But whispered low: "Pray let me go,
    I am a Demo-pop."

He sat there peering through the gate
    Till day wound up her golden yarn,
Into a ball and let it fall
    That God the star-worn sky might darn.
He spoke no word and made no fight,
    He knew not whither he would go;
He was not bent for tournament,
    Nor field where traitors' blood would flow.
He had no purpose in his chase,

He found it just as well to stop;
But ere he died he meekly cried:
   "I am a Demo-pop."

They dug his grave both wide and deep;
   And in the crisp November air,
With orgies grim, they buried him,
   And left him softly sleeping there.
His armor, made of burnished brass,
   Contained no message to a friend;
Upon his face there was no trace
   Of what had brought him to the end.
So on a slab of humble pine
   They wrote: "O, passing stranger, drop
A tear or so before you go,
   Here lies (no joke) a Demo-pop."

(Kansas City Journal, July 28, 1892. • 1. Portcullis. • 2. Democrat-Populist; the national "Populist" party was organized in 1891 and followed the general platform as the "People's Party," formed in Kansas in 1890.)

————

The Missouri Colonel
(Air from Pinafore)[1]
By Jingo[2]

The Missouri colonel is a soaring soul
   As free as a mountain bird;
His energetic fist is ready to resist
   A contradictory word.
Then his foot will stamp and his throat will growl,
His hair will twirl and his face will scowl,
His eyes will flash and his breast protrude,
And this then is his customary attitude.

35

When office he is after, which is every year,
 He's a different man indeed;
His fascinating smile is with him all the while,
 When his cause he goes to plead.
Then he travels o'er the country with his passes on the cars,[3]
He kisses all the babies and flatters their mammas.
He wheedles all the voters and his voice is never rude,
And this is then his customary attitude.

But when he is elected and the office holds,
 He resumes his native style;
Though if you've got a fee you'll very soon see
 He is after it all the while.
'Tis a fee for this and a fee for that
And a fee for the other, and he waxes fat,
For the state pays his rent and it buys his food,
And this is then his customary attitude.

But wait till next November and then you'll see
 A change come o'er his dreams;
For Warner's[4] about and will throw them out,
 As sure as morning gleams.
Then his head will hang and his shoulders stoop,
And his nose will snivel and his eyes will droop,
And his voice will quaver and his lip protrude,
And this will be his everlasting attitude.

(Kansas City Journal, August 7, 1892. • 1. "H.M.S. Pinafore" by Sir William Schwenck Gilbert (1836-1911) and Sir Arthur Seymour Sullivan (1842-1900). • 2. Here used as a jocular oath, not as a pseudonym. • 3. Politicians were given free railroad passes in the days when railroads needed political support; newspaper editors and major reporters also received free passes for political favors in the press. • 4. Major William Warner was the current Democratic governor of Missouri.)

(Untitled)

The battle in its fury raged
    Among the hills of Maine;
Each general his contest waged
    With might of brawn and brain.
The nation's eyes were centered on
    The outcome of the fray;
For as a die 'twould prophesy
    The end another day.
No word then uttered JAMES G.B.[1]
    But hacked a troubled cough,
And saved, you'll note,
Both "time and vote,"
    So Jim paired off.[2]

What cared he for the shaky fence,
    The campaign drums and flutes?
" 'Tis really of no consequence,"
    Said Jeems, with Mr. Toots.
"Let those who want to, worry;
    'Tis not my day, and then,
Somehow this year my time is dear,
    Give my regards to Ben.
"Tell Carter not to fret himself."
    He laughed a little laff
And hove a sigh
And wank an eye
    And Jim paired off.

(*Kansas City Star,* September 21, 1892. • 1. James Gillespie Blaine (January 31, 1830-January 27, 1893) was a statesman, Secretary of State in two cabinets, Speaker of the House for three terms, Senator from Maine for years, and once a candidate for the Presidency. • 2. "Paired off," to agree with one of the opposite political party to abstain from voting.)

A Saga of "de Sixt"[1]

It was in Doolan's wassail[2] hall this doughty deed was done,
    O Higgins is a farmer, mama, isn't he pie?[3]
And gathered there were "Foxy," Tim O'Toole and "Slicky" Dunn
    But Gehagan is a looloo,[4] an' that's no lie.

O a scurvy knight was Higgins with his homemade armor on,
    O Higgins is a farmer, mama, isn't he pie?
Then up spoke he to Doolan, "And where hath Gehagan gone?"
    But Gehagan was a looloo, say, and that's no lie.

"O Gehagan hath besworn himself to meet me here at nine"
    An' it's Higgins is a farmer, mama, isn't he pie?
"And pay to me some sesterces[5] he borrowed all so fine;"
    But Gehagan is a looloo, say, an' that's no lie.

Then long and loud laughed Doolan, "Slicky," "Foxy " and O'Toole
    For Higgins is a farmer, mama, isn't he pie?
And beguyed[6] the stranger chevalier and named him for a fool
    Yes, Gehagan is a looloo, say, an' that's no lie.

Full wroth was Higgins in his spleen, but never word quoth he
    For Higgins is a farmer, mama, isn't he pie?
Nor drank from the wassail bowl they passed about in glee
    O Gehagan is a looloo, say, an' that's no lie.

Then spoke up Doolan tauntingly, "O I'll lay thee wager[7] fair"
    For Higgins is a farmer, mama, isn't he pie?
"Gehagan will not meet thee here to keep the vow he sware;"
    O Gehagan is a looloo, say, an' that's no lie.

(Undated. William Allen White Library, Emporia State University. Reprinted with permission of Barbara White Walker. • 1. Probably the political sixth-ward boundary in Kansas City, Missouri, as shown on ward and precinct boundaries on maps in the *Kansas City Star,* November 7, 1892; February 19, 1894 and April 2, 1894. The sixth ward contained precincts 25-29. • 2. A saloon. • 3. A saucy, wily or cunning person. • 4. Colloquial for strange antics of thought or behavior. • 5. An ancient Roman coin equal to one-quarter of a denarius. • 6. Beguiled, i.e., to delude by guile; to deceive. • 7. A bet.)

The Returns on "de Row"[1]

If youse must yell for Grover,[2] go an' hunt another place,
An' don't git gay about it er I beat yer in de face.
Dey's plenty other marks was hit roun' hyur de same as me,
An' funny Cleveland talk don't go wid us dis evenun. See?
Wot t'ell I chewun of de rag fer? Say, I'se one dem chunks
Wot puts me wad on Benny[3] so I lose ten plunks.

We lose when Billy Myer before Jack McAuliffe fell,
We lose when Jimmy Corbett put de kibosh to John L.[4]
We lose on craps like farmers, an' at ev'ry game we plays
We lose our sparks an' tickers like a lot of bloomun jays.
I easy pays de trimmuns on a dozen rotten drunks —
Den puts me wad on Benny an' I drops ten plunks.

Wot t'ell I care fer Cleveland when I got no overcoat?
Saw off dere on de tariff er I t'umps youse in de t'roat.
But den I learns dis lesson in my meek and lowly walks:
I never stakes another rod on anyt'hing wot walks.
Dat goes. An' now I hits one of dem twenty-five cent bunks[5] —
I puts me wad on Benny an' I drops ten plunks.

(Kansas City Star. November 9, 1892. • 1. "Battle Row" was the area along the west side of Main Street from 3rd to 5th — so named because of all the fights that spilled out of the saloons that lined the streets. • 2. Stephen Grover Cleveland (1837-1908), 22nd and 24th President of the U.S. in 1885-1889 and 1893-1897. • 3. Benjamin Harrison (1833-1901), 23rd President of the U.S., 1889-1893. • 4. Myer, McAuliffe, Corbett and John L. Sullivan — all boxers. • 5. Flop-house beds.)

"Col. Hucks"[1] on Col. Harris [2]

I've just got this week's *Banner*[3], ma, an' I been readun some
About the way the 'lection went, as I was drivun home.
Ol' Cleveland's[4] got in, mother, 'spite of all the boys could do,
An' tuck the hull thing with him; so they carried Kansas, too.
Yes, Comrade Smith is beaten, and O, mother, shed a tear
For Kansas sends to congress, ma, a rebel brigadier!
O for a man like ol' John Brown,[5] in this dark hour of need,
Whose body lies a mould'run, but whose soul has stopped to feed.

How quick the times are changun, ma, ol' Kansas hain't the state
She was back in the loyil days that closed with eighty-eight;
When John J.[6] skinned the rebels, an' ol' Plumb[7] come chargun thro'
The ranks of Union Labor like he knew the way to do.
We used to have bean dinner then, camp fires an' barbycues,
An' in our dictionary they was no sich word as fuse.[8]
They wan't no talk of rebels then, for John Brown was our creed —
Whose body may lie mould'run, but whose soul has stopped to feed.

It hain't as if one deestric', ma, could bear the awful charge
Of sendun up a rebel — 'tis the hull darn state-at-large.
Was it for this I suffered down on Mississippi's shore?
Was it for this the hoppers come, way back in semty-four?
Oh, mother, what would Abner say, if he could wake him up?
And what would Lige and Ezry do a dreenun of this cup?
Was it for this ol' John Brown fit, and made poor Kansas bleed?
Which his body lies a mould'run, but his soul has stopped to feed.

I guess the Word[9] will help me some — I find it always does.
Then, ma, read out the story of the "perfect man"[10] of Uz,
Who when he lost his livestock, an' the childern of his race,
He fainted not, ner backslid, through the mortgage took the place.
Then let us with our potsherds[11] scrape our sores like Job an' say:
The Lord gave Kansas glory once; the Lord can take away.
An' maybe Job will punch John up, an' maybe he'll take heed —
Whose body lies a mould'run, whilst his soul has stopped to feed.

(*Kansas City Star,* November 12, 1892. • 1. "Col. Hucks" was a rarely used pseud-
onym of White, but there was a Colonel William Hucks of the Upper Slate Creek in
Center township who was elected as a delegate to the State Republican League con-
vention in Topeka. • 2. Colonel William Alexander Harris (1841-*ca.* December 10,
1909) was a pioneer breeder of Scottish shorthorns, and ran against George T. An-
thony for congressman-at-large, which he won. He was later a U.S. Senator, and was
appointed Regent of Kansas State College by Kansas Governor Stubbs. • 3. White
often referred to an imaginary newspaper as the *Banner,* see his *A Certain Rich Man,*
p. 59 ... the *Sycamore Ridge Banner.* • 4. Stephen Grover Cleveland (1837-1908),
24th President of the U.S. • 5. John Brown (1800-1859), American abolitionist. • 6.
John James Ingalls (1833-1900). • 7. Preston Bierce Plumb (1837-1891). • 8. Short
for "fusion" — the Kansas legislative term for any elected member whose party alle-
giance was not strictly Democrat or Republican. • 9.-10. The Holy Bible. • 11. A piece
of fragment of a broken earthen pot.

Jim Didn't Worry

Nobody never quite made out Jim;[1]
    'Peared like they allers just thought him queer,
And kinder cranky and laughed at him
    When Jim would tell 'em he didn't keer.
"Don't make no dif'er'nce," I've heerd him say,
    An' most folks called him a jolly brick —
"It's a tough ol' world, an 'll have its way;
    'Taint worryin' me — I've got no kick."

But I knowed better; he's come to me
    Many's the time heartsick an' sore;
"I'm tired of the whole outfit," sez he,
    "They ain't no use ever tryin' no more;"
An' then in a crowd he'd perk up smart,
    An' sorter sneer at the deals he'd git;
"That? That's nothing'! W'y bless your heart,
    I ain't a worryin' a little bit."

Jim *was* unlucky, no use to talk;
    Folks wondered sometimes at the way he done,
But I know why he used to balk

41

An' give up suthin' he'd just begun.
    His back had been broke by circumstance,
        An' allers unlucky, he'd los' his grit;
    But still he'd laugh — "I ain't had no chance,
        But *I* ain't a-worryin' a little bit."

So Jim went a laughin' right down to death,
    An' he let go o' life not keerin' a darn;
"Pardner," sez he, kinder catchin' his breath,
    As I set watchin', with the night on the turn,
"I hain't had much of a deal down here,
    And I ain't askin' now for a softer sit;
I'm jest a-lettin' go, bend lower, d'ye hear?
    I *ain't* — worryin' now — not — a — little — bit."

(Kansas City Star, December 8, 1892. • 1. White's dislike for James Gillespie Blaine (1830-1893) describes reasons why the average American citizen would show little sadness when Blaine died a few months later.)

——

"Danny Deever" Up to Date

"What is your bugle blowin' for?" said Rudyard to the maid.
"To turn you out, to turn you out," the colored servant said.
"What makes you look so pale and white?" said Rudyard to the maid."
"I'm dreadin' what I've got to watch," the colored servant said..
For they're up with Baby Kipling, you can hear the swear words play;
The family's in a hollow square[1] — they're up with her to-day,
She's driven of the neighbors off for seven blocks away,
    An' they're up with Baby Kipling in the mornin'.

"What makes 'er breathe so loud an' hard?" said Rudyard-on-parade.
"It's gotter cold, it's gotter cold," the colored servant said.
For they're up with Baby Kipling, Daddy's marchin' her around;
An' they've 'alted Baby Kipling while her daddy's toe is bound,

42

An' she'll yowl in 'alf a minute like a homeless, friendless 'ound —
  Oh, they're up with Baby Kipling in the mornin'.

"Er cot is right 'and cot to mine," said Rudyard-on-parade.
"She ain't sleepin' much to-night," the colored servant said.
"I give 'er pap[2] a score of times," said Rudyard-on-parade.
"She's weepin' bitter tears all right" the colored servant said.
They're up with Baby Kipling, you must walk 'er 'round the place,
For there's somethin' on her stomach, and there's wrath upon 'er face,
An' she's 'owlin' like a Fejee[3] to 'er quiet dad's disgrace —
  While they're up with Baby Kipling in the mornin'.

"What makes 'er grow black in the face?" says Rudyard-on-parade.
"She's yelping so she's lost 'er wind," the colored servant said.
"What's that a-breakin' over 'ead?" said Rudyard-on-parade.
"It is the welcome rosy morn,' the colored servant said.
For they're done with Baby Kipling, Papa now can run an' play,
She's peacefully a-sleepin' an' the doctor's gone away,
An' tootsey, you can bet you'll drive your dad to drink to-day,
  After bein' up with baby in the morning.

(Undated, but written for the *Kansas City Star* in humorous jest for poet Rudyard
Kipling (1865-1936). Also entitled, "Kipliana Domestica," it appears in the William
Allen White Collection, Emporia State University Library; reprinted with permis-
sion of Barbara White Walker. "Danny Deever" was Kipling's poem published in the
Scotts Observer, February 22, 1890 — the first in a series of "Barrack-Room Ballads."
White here imitates Kipling's use of the ballad form and employs the recurrence of
the same end-words which suggest the routine and exhaustive care of Kipling's first-
born daughter — Josephine Kipling, born December 29, 1892, in Brattleboro, Ver-
mont. • 1. Comparable to the British infantry's tactical-defense position. • 2. A soft
food for infants and invalids. • 3. Figian members of the native race of the Figi Is-
lands whose ceremonial dances require loud shouts.)

Our Distinguished Visitors

The Nizam of Hyderabad and the Nawab of Rampoor
With the dusky maharajas of Bhawnagar and Johore,
And the Gaekwar of Baroda and the Ramee of Gendal,
With the Raja of Travancore and the Begum of Bhopal,
Are headed for Chicago,[1] and there'll be a pretty muss
When we try to address them and they try to speak with us;
And what a crash of consonants in Jackson Park will fling
When Mr. Higganbotham meets Raja Jajajit Singh.

Come and tell us, Maharaja, Nawab, Gaekwar and Nizam,
All about your young man Kipling,[2] living with your Uncle Sam.
Have you ever met Mulvaney, "sarjint" once, but "since rejuced?"
Are they true, those famous stories telling how he ruled the roost?
Tell us one thing, tell us truly, do your fakirs really make
All the things the *menasahibs* say, or do the latter fake?
Is human nature molded on your hills and in your *rukh*
In another pair of molds than those we use — say, at Dubuque?

Come, be honest now and tell us, if a man from Kohlapur
Should come over to Chicago and relate things as they were —
Fuddling you with foreign phrases, would you not give up the fight,
And fork over all his laurels rather than contest his right?
And suppose he made his hero hail from Walla Walla, Wash.,
And described a blondined heroine residing at Oshkosh,
Then suppose he talked of sea-things, telling in an airy way
How "the dawn comes up like thunder" from Muskegon 'cross the bay—."

Would you confess your ignorance and damn it out of hand?
Or would you join the crowd and say: "Of course, we understand?"
For if you'd take the latter course, we Saxons can forget
The saddle color of your skin and make you brothers yet.
For, oh, it is our weakness and our glory and our pride
That if we do not catch the joke we're always keen to hide
Our ignorance, and crown the man who puzzled us beside.

(Kansas City Star, July 28, 1893; • 1. President Grover Cleveland opened the World's
Fair in Chicago on Monday, May 1, 1893. Many foreign dignitaries attended the open-
ing ceremonies in a salute to the procession of nations which hailed the progress of
the new world. • 2. Rudyard Kipling (1865-1936), English author.)

Election Day on Willer Crick

Election day on Willer Crick — the carriages are out,
The dollars on the candidates are fluttering about:
There's seegars at the post office with all the feller's cards,
Besides a keg of Evan's beer down at the railroad yards.
The Methodists are giving dinner in the Pirtle block,
And old man Carey's cider mill is up from Little Rock —
But as I started in to say, I'll say, now I've begun,
Election day on Willer Crick is where you get your fun.

Bill Hoy behind the feed store, with his haunches on his heels,[1]
Is laying off his thus and so to little painter Peals —
Explaining in an undertone how all the township slates
Are fixed for him in combine with the stalwart candidates;
Old Redden, he walks knowingly about and clears his throat,
And smiles and tucks his right hand in his double-breasted coat;
While E.N. Smith is caging 'round, now jumping in his rig,
Now piling out and swearing like he owns the thing-my-jig.

There — looking shrewd and feeling he's the smoothest man in town —
"Doc" Armstrong goes tiptoeing, seegar up and hat brim down.
Abe Leidy's Boy from Glencoe says his pap says all is fine,
And won't we send ten dollars more to keep the boys in line?
The women folks make errands down and sidle past the polls,
And ask the grocery clerk how is it going with Lafe Knowles.
The children want the mail at least a dozen times a day,
And though there's been no train in, they keep coming anyway.

Old Sap, the blacksmith, he's come out togged in his army blue,
And him and Colyer, Hicks and Hobbs are working for La Rue.
Old Vandy's drunk and dressed up, but he doesn't care a lick.
He'll drive home standing up and yell until he's crost the crick.
The Bemis boys have come to town, a spilin' for a fight,
And 'Kige, he's in the calaboose where Link'll be by night.
I make no doubt there's grander scenes when nobler deeds are done —
But Willer Crick election day is where you get your fun.

(Kansas City Star, November 6, 1893. • 1. "Hunkered down" as they now say.)

Free Silver and Free Trade

The campaign now is started and the "pops" are getting thick.
Free Silver is the issue and 'tis talked till one is sick.
The Democrats and pops are mixed into a silver stew,
But just who'll get elected I cannot guess, can you?
The orators are shouting for free silver and for gold,
The pops are laughing at the way the Democrats they sold,
And Bryan he is certain to the White House he will go,
While McKinley's just as certain Bryan hasn't any show.

Four years ago they told us they would give us lots of dust
And we wouldn't have to labor, if in Free Trade we would trust,
And they told us that our troubles and our cares would soon be over
If we'd do just as they told us and cast our vote for Grover,
And they partly kept their bargain, but they made us all believe
That we wouldn't have to labor for our wants we would receive;
Oh, we do not have to labor, not a stroke we've done begot
Since Grover got elected — for we cannot get a job.

And they tell us that free silver will give us better times.
We'll have lots of money in dollars, halves and dimes,
But how they're going to work it is not yet clear to me;
It may be a repetition of free trade and Grover C.
As I sit here just a thinking of the hardships I've come through
And figuring and thinking just what I ought to do.
The days are mighty gloomy, but they would be much blacker
So I'll vote for Bill McKinley if it costs me my terbacker.

(Emporia Gazette, October 27, 1896.)

The Truth About the Gineril

"Sez Bill Bryan[1] to Joe Bur-r-ton[2], 'Ave yez saw the Gineril?"
'Phwat Gineril?' sez Joe Bur-r-ton.
'Generil Prosperity,' sez Bill Bryan, laffin fit to kill.
For ut was considered a good joke in thim days."
                                   — William Jennings Bryan, *The First Battle*

Oh Oi 'ave saw the Generil: he's lookin' vury well;
He's ridin' in the cushion chairs and livin' loike a swell.
On the door mats of the farmers are the photos of his fate
An' he's dropped the money question while he's talkin' dollar whate.[3]
Oh, the Gineril's a sly old dog, just listen to the cans
A-rattlin' in the milk house where he's gone to find the pans.
Oh, he's flirtin' wid the farmer's wife an' huggin' all her girls,
An' givin' thim the notion they're too good for jukes and earls.
Oh, Gineril just take the brist:[4] the dark mate and the wing.
        We have no band to grate you,
        But we're mighty glad to mate you,
        An' you bet we're go'n' to trate you
Loike the scion[5] ava king.

Oh, Gineril, we're sorry you was druv[6] here by distress —
By the famine that's in Injy[7] an' in Europe more or less.
We're sorry for the shortage that has come in Injun whate,
We're sorry for the Injun hogs that makes our bacon on swate,
We're sorry for the Injun steers in Injun cattle pens,
We're sorry for the Injuns stroike that's shut down Injun hens,
An' the Gineril he snickered as he tuk a hunk of pie,
        An' he never said a worrud[8]
        That ony av us herrud[9]
        But the Gineril's a burrud[10]
— So he wunk the other eye.

An' Gineril, you say you've come to visit quite a while
Then it's here's lookin' at you as we have a little smile.
Don't feel that you are company; just feel at home an' free
To eat a cold snack in the night — like one of the familee.

For you are our old army frind an', Gineril, we know
The best we have is none too good to make yer fwuskers grow.
And while ye drill the tarriers[11] at work these gloryus days,
> Remember that we love ye
> An' as sure's the sky's above ye
> We'll bust the ear drum av ye
A hollerin' yer praise.

(Emporia Gazette, September 18, 1897. • 1. White here elaborates upon Bryan's joke, in which Democrats thought it funny to ask Republicans what President William McKinley would do as a proponent of a protective tariff and sound money (gold standard). Bryan, defeated by McKinley in the 1896 election, was a Democrat who ran on the ticket of free silver. • 2. Joseph Ralph Burton (1852-1923), Senator from Kansas, was sent to jail for irregular practices. • 3. One bushel of wheat was worth $1.00. • 4. The breast. • 5. The son of a king, a prince. • 6. Driven. • 7. India. • 8. A word. • 9. Heard. • 10. Bird; a sign of disapproval to general prosperity that President McKinley had used as an election campaign. • 11. Terriers, i.e., to train Washington bureaucrats as dogs.)

Sing Without Further Lining

How dear to my heart is the old-fashioned snorter,[1] who roamed over Kansas two short years ago; who thirsted for gore and fancied he'd orter, hang all the plutocrats up in a row. Oh, where are "the downtrodden millions a starving," where is "the increasing army of tramps," and where is the man who yearned for the carving, where and, oh, where is that bad case of cramps? The old-fashioned snorter, the blood-blowing snorter, the man-eating snorter that Kansas once grew; has vanished, departed, in fact, he has sorter, lit out and skipped to the tra la la loo. He's left us, but Kansans are hardly the losers; he's drowned in the deluge of prosperity; the rights of the owner are more than the users, and for some time to come they are likely to be. So here drop a tear for the old-fashioned snorter, whom, let us all pray, we may ne'er again meet; then pause and remember the silver exhorter, whose sides were bulged in when he monkeyed with wheat. Oh, the old-fashioned snorter, the Populist snorter, the wild wooly snorter we once knew so well, today can be purchased at six for a quarter, down in the cinder department of hell.

(Emporia Gazette, March 8, 1898. • 1. Anyone strikingly violent, noisy or intense.)

Insurgents

O come my love, insurge with me, adown the bosky dell; we'll chase
the nimble octopus across the barren fell; the moon is high, the
tariff, too, is rising every hour; so come, my love, insurge with me,
here in my sylvan bower. Yes, come, my love, and trip with me the
light fantastic toe; and as we slip along let's trip our agile Uncle
Joe. The differentials are in bloom, the ad valorem beams; the rules
are moaning at the bar, while dimpled freedom screams. Then come,
my love, let us insurge; Ah let us rage and snorts: O let us paw the
soft lush grass, while our two hearts cavort. The time is ripe, the
hour is here, our sone will be no dirge; O let us whoop and fly the
coop — come on — O let's insurge.

(Emporia Gazette, December 10, 1909; a "machine poem?)*

Battle Hymn of Empory

O the voters rose and snorted, and they ripped the shingles loose!
And the voters pawed and gamboled, and they surely raised the doose!
And we might go round in sackcloth, but, O thunder, what's the use?
        Empory marches on!

O the bulwarks may be busted, and the sweet beans may be canned,
And perhaps we ought to bellow till our wailings filled the land;
But a better time's a-coming and we'll whoop to beat the band —
        Empory marches on!

The town will be a humming as it hummed the year before;
We'll all be fat and happy, with a stand-off at the store;
And the man who needs a kicking is the one whose head is sore —
        Empory marches on!

(Emporia Gazette, April 6, 1910)*

And Now in Conclusion

I'm weary and tired and sad at seeing the candidate's face, smirking or scowling like mad, from every imaginable place. I'm down on the pesky straw vote; at circular letters I'm hot; I gag at the clarion note and boiling political pot. I'm glad that my country is saved and baled up and carted away. I don't givadam who is laved[1] by the billows of Salt Creek[2] today. So take me far out of the town, away where the roorback[3] can't roam; where boomerangs never drop down, nor keynotes[4] nor cards make their home. O had I a Zep'lin[5] I'd fly to some shiny cold desert star, away from the candidate's lie, away from the candidate's car. For I am weary and sore, my feet hurt, my teeth ache, I'm sick, I've sure got the willys[6] and more, so let me go jump in the crick.

(Emporia Gazette, November 3, 1914. • 1. To wash or bathe. • 2. Salt Creek (see also "A Free Salt River Trip"); a political expression of the winning opposition to give an imaginary concession to the losing candidate. • 3. A defamatory falsehood published for political effect. • 4. An address, as at a political convention, that presents the essential issues of interest to the assembly. • 5. A rigid airship of a type first constructed in 1899-1900 by Ferdinand Count von Zeppelin (1838-1917). • 6. Willies; slang, a fit of nervousness).

Hope Beyond

There are more or less tears being silently shed,
    Bemoaning us three;
And more or less written and more or less said,
Assuming that we are all more or less dead —
    Victor[1] and Henry[2] and me.[3]

Now I have arisen to say it ain't so,
    Concerning us three.
We're very much hitched to the earth here below;
Our wings haven't sprouted and we shall not go;
We're still her to kick at the old status quo,
    Henry and Victor and me.

It's true we are out on the end of the limb,
    All of us three.
It's true that our chances to climb down are slim;
And also, our chance to go upward is dim;
But the scenery's splendid up where we have climb —
    Victor and Henry and me.

The society's good and the weather is calm,
    For all of us three.
And each of us feels as serene as a clam.
If politics skids, or a wheel slips a kam
Oh, what do we care — not a tinker's red dam;
    Henry nor Victor, nor me.

We're naturally touched by your tribute of tears,
    Is each of us three.
But do not give way to your anguish or fears;
We're fuller of ginger than two-year-old steers,
And ain't been so happy for seventeen years,
    Victor and Henry and me.
        Because you see
        By geemunee,
        We're free — per se,
        Victory and Henry and me.

My moral conclusion, must make it clear why,
    In naming us three,
It had to be "me" when it should have been "I."
It's that we Bull Moosers[4] are so mortal shy,
We wished to avoid, even rhyming with pie[5] —
    So it's Henry and Victor and me!

(Emporia Gazette, May 22, 1915; *Topeka Daily Capital,* May 23, 1915. Familiarly
known as "Victor, Henry and Me," this poem was originally delivered before the Sat-
urday Night Literary Club of Topeka, November 28, 1914. • 1. Victor Murdock (1871-
1945), nominated for U.S. Senator, and was chairman of the Progressive party. • 2.
Henry J. Allen (1868-1950) was a barber and newspaper publisher who was unwit-
tingly elected to Governor of Kansas while overseas with White during WWI. He was
also appointed to the U.S. Senate after Charles Curtis became vice president. • 3.
William Allen White. • 4. Members of the Progressive party and followers of Theodore
Roosevelt, in 1912. • 5. A mixed, jumbled mess.)

Some Fragmentary Thoughts
on How to Run a Country Town
and Make a Living at It

Knock and the town knocks on you,
Boost and you fill your pouch.
The town has room
For the men who boom,
But it's too blame small for the grouch.

Kick and your own pants feel it;
Pull and you'll have your say.
When you trade at home,
You are going some,
But not when you send away.

Teamwork nails down ducats,[1]
And ducats that stay in town
Make yens[2] and rocks
That build brick blocks,
Where they jingle and settle down.

But ducats that roll to the city
Fill the home town with hate;
They take men's jobs
And they break off gobs
Of the spirit that makes towns great.

So boost for your local merchant
Through fair and cloudy weather.
Those towns don't rust
Nor go ker-bust
Where folks all pull together.

* * * * *

These few lines are written for the Emporia Trade Week, in the fond
hope that they will get somewhere.

(Emporia Gazette, September 23, 1915. • 1. A gold coin of several European coun-
tries. • 2. A Japanese monetary unit.)

A B.-D. Day

O, what will you drink when the bone-dry bill[1]
    Is part of the law of the land?
Alas, and I'll swig till I get my fill —
    Some soapsuds sweetened with sand.
And where will you drink when the bone-dry law
    Has put up the bars for you?
I'll hie me down to the raging Kaw
    And make me some catfish stew!

I'll make me a catfish stew, by heck,
    With catnip tea for grog;
And I'll pour me down my arid neck
    The juice of a catalogue.[2]
A catalogue of dear red-eye,
    That bloomed in the olden time.
When rock and rye went sousing by
    To the jig-jag's[3] mellow chime.

I've a bone-dry taste in my bone-dry mouth,
    And a bone-dry tear in my lamp.[4]
For these be the days of the bone-dry drouth
    Which I don't give a bone-dry damp![5]

Nary a bode-dry damp gib I,
    For butch too butch id sad.
      With bug-juice gone,
      Whad shall we pud on,
    A cold id a bode-dry head?

(*Emporia Gazette,* February 23, 1917. • 1. The "bone-dry" liquor bill, passed by the Kansas legislature on January 31, 1917, prohibited possession of liquor, and imposed a $500 fine and six-months imprisonment for its violation. White heartily endorsed the bill because it required removal of liquor from drug stores and prohibited its sale for any reason — including medical. • 2. A descriptive list of beers, wines and liquors. • 3. Enough alcohol to make one noticeably drunk. • 4. Only his tear of remorse remains in his drinking vessel. • 5. Damn.)

The Ballade of the Ghosts

"Alas, I was born too early,
    And alack, I had no chance,"
And he backed him up
To a thunderbold,
    Which merrily kicked his pants.
"I am the wraith[1] of Jesse James,[2]
    A robber both bold and free,
By the great horn spoon[3]
I died too soon
    What a profiteer I'd be.

"Oh bring me some thin milk gruel,[4]
    "I have lost my taste for blood.
"The things I see
On earth make me
    Ashamed I was Robin Hood."
And the ghost sobbed two feet of rain,
    And gave a whole county a souse,[5]
And sighed: "If I could
"Go to Arden Wood[6]
    I'd set up a packing house!"

"Say, boy, fetch me a halo
    And daub it with golden paint;
And you tell the world
Which below us has whirled
    That I am a blushing saint!
Which I was a pirate once on earth
    And maybe was morally queer,
But Captain Kidd[7]
Takes off his lid
    To the modern profiteer."

And three wraiths buried their heads in clouds,
    And bawled till the thunder riz.
And Kidd he bolted a lightening stew,
And James took the same and Hood took two,

And they went out on an astral wizz.
For they were just amateur robbers,
And never the equals or peers,
They were only poor lunks
Compared with the skunks
We have branded as profiteers.

(*Emporia Gazette,* September 5, 1919. • 1. A ghost. • 2. Jesse Woodson James (1847-1882), American outlaw and legendary figure, born in Centerville (now Kearney), Clay County, Missouri. • 3. A superlative oath. • 4. A thin porridge made by boiling a cereal in water or milk. • 5. To drench or wet thoroughly. • 6. A forested region in France and Belgium where heavy fighting occurred during World War I. • 7. Captain William Kidd (*ca.* 1645-1701), British pirate and privateer.)

Pay Up

The railroad strike has passed us, and the rates are coming down. We have joy enough to last us, till we get our harp and crown. So let's telescope our faces; firmly cork our briney tears. Let us hit the giddy paces of them olden golden years. Let us drink the fizzy water that is sparkling in the cup; but before we drink we orter celebrate by paying up! Let us pay the gentle grocer, and the coal man and the Doc. Let us ask him what we owe sir, then plank down upon the block, all our ducats, bones and dollars, all our sestences[1] and beans; let us shed our shirts and collars and our B.V.D.'s[2] and jeans. Let us straighten our relations, though the process may seem rough; let us strip our obligations, till we come down to the buff. Every time we shove a dollar, out to pay an honest debt, we can hear the Eagle[3] holler, we can see the Goddess[4] sweat. So pay up, you frisky fellows, who have let your credit go! Pay up now before it mellows; it may rot before you know. Dig although you kill the kiddies, starve your wife and sell the pup. Your one best eternal bid is — Man, for Heaven's sake pay up.

(*Emporia Gazette,* October 28, 1921. The Lyon County Retailers' Association currently pleaded with creditors to pay overdue monthly accounts. • 1. A misspelling of *sesterce,* a Roman coin of silver (later brass) equal to one-fourth *denarius.* • 2. Company name for product line of underclothing founded by Bradley, Voorhees and Day. • 3. Coins of American mintage impressed with an eagle. • 4. American coins imprinted with Lady Liberty.)

The Animal Fair

"Democrats Going Wet Next Year and G.O.P. Hopes to Capture West with Dry Plank." — *Newspaper headlines*

Come listen to my ditty and try to check your tears
The donkey of Democracy has fins instead of ears,
His hoofs have sprouted duck webs and his lungs have turned to gills,
And the donkey is a hootch hound now whose guts are copper stills.

And now behold the elephant has swiped the camel's hump.
The elephant has bitten every bar keep on the rump.
The elephant has signed the pledge; no more will he get drunk
But peddle tracts and moral saws[1] and sermons from his trunk.

(Emporia Gazette, January 8, 1923. • 1. A saying or proverb)

Kansas on Guard

The world may wobble, sway and rock, the earth may trip and reel,
the universe may faint with shock and stagger on its keel; the
cosmos may devour its tail and revert to a dream, the dream may
wane, dissolve and pale, and leave no sign or gleam. But in the
wreck and waste of space, the sad collapse of time, one point shall
hold its ancient grace, its dignity sublime. And there sweet
seraphim[1] shall come, and clap their gleeful hands, and chortle
through the vacuum, "See Kansas, there she stands!"

(Emporia Gazette, March 28, 1923; Ted McDaniel, managing editor of the *Gazette* in
1962, remembered this prose-poem of White's. On the U.S. Senate floor, only one lone
member — Senator Charles Curtis of Kansas — was present when the gavel fell
calling the Senate to order. The call bells clamored for a prolonged period before a
quorum appeared. • 1. The seraphim are ranked as the highest order of angels,
immediately above the cherubim.)

We Tune in with Charley[1]

The springtime is here, gentle Annie, the fruit trees are in bloom, the bass are biting, the farmers are plowing and planting, everybody went to church Easter Sunday who wanted to go, everybody who wants to assemble peaceably may go ahead and do it (provided he is willing to let his neighbor see his face[2] while he is doing it), anybody who wants to petition congress for a redress of grievances may go ahead and petition, (however little good it may do him), and by and large it is a bully[3] good old world for everybody to live in — except the men who take themselves too seriously!
> — Charles F. Scott, editorial in *The Iola Register.)*

Down!
Left!
Right!
Up!
SING!

The sap is in the senior and his papa's in the red. The Kluxer[4] blows his sawbuck[5] and is crazy in the head. The candidate is canning guff[6] and kidding of himself. Vox populi[7] is popping like the hootch[8] upon the shelf. So let us all be happy and cavort and whoop and sing. The world is on a festive toot. The year is at the spring. Oh let us lift our voices and our hearts unto the skies, and catch up with our taxes as they magnify and rise. For life is full of happiness; and joy is full of tunes and who would sigh and beef and cry is full of doleful prunes. Amen!

(Emporia Gazette, April 25, 1924. • 1. Charles F. Scott of *The Iola Register.* • 2. Ku Klux Klan members always wore hoods and masks and white overcloaks to avoid identity. • 3. Well done! Bravo! • 4. A KKK member. • 5. A ten-dollar bill. • 6. i.e., taking a lot of criticism. • 7. Voice of the people. • 8. Destroying wines and liquors during Prohibition times.)

Some Vagrant Thoughts on the Ground Hog

The Ground Hog seen his shadder at just one-eighteen today, and he clumb down the ladder to his hole and slunk away. For forty days the weather is a-coming cold and dreer; just the same, no matter whether you complain or rise and cheer. For the Ground Hog he has said it, and he never grinned or smiled; so he'll now proceed to edit this month's weather, raw and wild. Of course, we do not like it; of course, we'd like to kick; and of course, we'd like to strike it from the calendar d. quick. But other things have risen which have made our biler burst;[1] so the Ground Hog knows that hisen[2] is not totally the worst. There's the Democratic party, and there's two more years of it; with the standpats[3] hale and hearty, which that doesn't help a bit! Cyclones, earthquakes, freaks of nature — floods and drouths pass one by one, and the Kansas legislature still has thirty days to run. So be gentle with the Ground Hog, for he might be twice as bad; thank the Lord it ain't the hound dog of Champ Clark[4] we might have had. For when man's a-seekin' trouble and is grouchin' at his lot, Old Man Grief just mixes double — pell to hay and no pitch hot! So, let's pet the little critter who keeps weather in his trunk; glad he does not have the bitter end that permeates the skunk!

(*Emporia Gazette,* February 2, 1915. • 1. The viscid fluid secreted by the liver. • 2. Even the ground hog's gloomy prediction is incomparable to the Democrat's dubious legislation. • 3. A political policy characterized by doing nothing. • 4. James Beauchamp Clark, speaker of the Democratic House, who lost the nomination for President at the national convention.)

———

Wilson

God gave him a great vision
The devil gave him an imperious heart.
The proud heart is still
The vision lives.

(*Emporia Gazette,* February 4, 1924; a blank verse obituary poem about Woodrow Wilson {1856-1924}, 28th President of the United States.)

Canton and Cleveland

These faces young and comely are not smiling, they are bent
In those uncanny postures by a frigid President.
His heart is ice, his hand is stone, his meditations grow
In forms of grotesque hoar frost and his dreams are drifted snow
And when these two lads struck the blast of his cold storage cheer
They took the train for Cleveland and they got the glad hand here.

(Everett Rich, *William Allen White; the man from Emporia.* New York: Farrar &
Rinehart, 1941, 95-96. Reprinted with permission from Henry Holt. White and his
publisher of *The Real Issue* {1896}, Chauncey L. Williams, were invited by Cleveland
businessman, Marcus Alonzo Hanna, to meet President-elect William McKinley at
Canton, Ohio. After receiving a cold reception from McKinley, both White and Will-
iams considered their icy meeting a frigid snub. White dashed off this poem to friends
in Cleveland, Ohio as a "victory " expression.)

HOLIDAYS

The Fourth of July

O what shall we do on the Fourth of July, said the youth to the maiden fair. O we'll take down the hammock and quickly hie, to the home of the chigger and dark green fly, where through leafy bowers the breezes sigh, and dream of our love out there. O what shall we do on the Fourth of July, said a youngster free from care.

O we'll fill up our systems with green apple pie and purchase toy pistols and then we'll try to blow out our souls to the homes in the sky, to sing with the angels fair. O what shall we do on the Fourth of July, the old codgers ask in despair. O we'll get a jug of Old Red Eye, and a gallon or two of rock and rye, and go out where there is nobody nye, and get on a great old tear. O what shall we do on the glorious Fourth, said the editor weary and tired. We'll stay at home in this day of mirth and boom the town for all 'tis worth. O we'll raise the price of our city's worth, although the boom's expired.

(*El Dorado Republican,* June 28, 1887; this "machine poem" appeared in White's column, "Saints and Sinners").

A Valentine

In those old days, the days now dead and sleeping,
In those old days the dream-world still is keeping,
In those old days, the days of young life's gladness,
In those old days so full of first love's madness.
In those old days — you recollect them, do you: —
In those old days I sang this love song to you:

The wind and the world may be cold to you, dear,
    Ho, bonnie maiden with eyes so blue,
For winds are as cruel as worlds are drear,
Then come to me, darling, with never a fear.
Come, come, come, sweetheart, come to me here,
    Ho, bonnie, cling to your true love.

And yet to-day heart throbs to heart no greeting;
And yet to-day we only bow at meeting;
And yet to-day in two graves love is moulding.
And yet to-day one past two hearts are holding;
And yet to-day by all the past worth living;
And yet, O friend! hear me and be forgiving.

                 South wind!
                 Soft wind!
             Kiss the hills again,
             Start the rills[1] again,
                 Soft wind!
                 South wind!

             Kiss and wake the sleeping spring,
               Till she pulses everything
           As when autumn's here,
           And the woods are sere[2]
And the passion of the summer's gone,
             Do the pensive days,
             Filled with April haze,
Seem to turn the year back to its dawn,
             So, my friend, may we,
             Strangers though we be —
Now that all love's fires are drenches for aye, —
             Kindly spring recall,
             And be friends for all —
Friends through all the Indian summer day.
                 Soft wind!
                 South wind!
           Kiss the hills again,
           Wake the spring, and then
           Waft the thorns and ashes all away.

(*Kansas City Star,* February 14, 1893; *Rhymes by Two Friends,* 215-16. • 1. Very small brooks. • 2. Dried-up, leafless.)

A Timely Valentine

This valentine is written for a little girl I know —
    Not for Clara, not for Lucy, nor for Jennie,
For a homely little maiden who has never had a beau,
    And hasn't even hopes of having any.

If I had lots of money I should write this rhyme in gold —
    Not for Nora, not for Susie, nor for Stella,
And seal it up with melted pearls, whose worth was never told,
    For the little girl who hasn't any fellow.

I'd fill it with a perfume sweeter than a baby's dream —
    Not for Mary, not for Ida, nor for Frances,
A dream pulled out like taffy, wrapped upon a love-star beam,
    For the girl who's been denied love's tender fancies.

I should fill it with such happy words as she would glow to hear —
    Not for Ella, not for Addie, nor for Kittie,
Words born of sweetest kisses, never heard by mortal ear —
    For the homely girl who never can be pretty.

God love that lonely maiden and be good to her this day —
    Not to Emma, not to Mildred, nor to Alice,
And bring her forth a knight, to chase the blue imps all away,
    And let her build an airy fairy palace.

So this valentine is written for a quiet little maid —
    Not for Lizzie, not for Rosa, nor for Celia,
To say to her: "Ho, ho, ah ah my I'm afraid! —
    Watch out for Master Cupid — or he'll steal you!"

(Kansas City Star, February 22, 1894.)

A Merry Christmas

For that the Lord gave His own Son to show us how to live
We celebrate the Christmas tide that we may learn to give;
That we may learn to give our hearts in daily sacrifice,
That we may learn what joy there is in service without price;
So here's a merry Christmas for all those who feel the touch
Of Lord Christ's hand upon them and have joy to suffer much;
For those who toil for others, for child or friend or kin,
Who bend to hard rough usage, who feel the grime of sin;
And if their eyes are blinded to God's deep moving will
E' en though they've lost Him in their work — a merry Christmas still!

For those whose hearts are fine and free, whose smiles reflect the sun,
For those who glow in beauty shedding light on every one,
For those who only feel the thrill of victors on the track,
From whom our Father's hand has kept His choicest blessing back;
For those poor souls unsorrowed, unwidowed and accurst
Who dream they have the best of life and only know the worst;
For those who see the roses and yet have no joy of tears,
For those who have no hallowed days in all the train of years;
For those whose eyes are blinded to God's deep moving will,
E'en though they've lost Him in their joy — a merry Christmas still!

For all of God's good creatures whom His broad purpose guides
Who burrow in the sullen earth or toil upon its tides;
For rich, for poor, for high, for low who labor in His name
For good, for bad, for gay or sad and those who live in shame;
For those His Holy Spirit moves to give themselves away,
E'en though they never feel His grace and have no heart to pray;
For those who've dropt their burdens and laid them down to rest
And left their work unfinished, unmeaning and unblest;
For those who lie and slumber in silence on the hill
Who found Him not until they slept — a merry Christmas still,
                    My Lord, a merry Christmas still!

(*Emporia Gazette,* December 25, 1910)

A Hymn for Thanksgiving

Our cities wax triumphant, all in clay and stone and steel,
Our fields are rich with provender, our bins are filled with meal.
The days have brought us glory and the year has brought us gold,
So come we to our temples as our fathers came of old.
We come with all our blessings; with all treasures that we hoard,
We come with joyous hearts to bring thanksgiving to our Lord.

Thou, Lord, whose might hath cherished us, Thou, who has filled our hands
With plenty, and hath brought us peace from all our sister lands —
O come thou, Lord, and mold our minds, and humble, Lord, our hearts,
So that we shall not glorify the milling in our marts.
Teach us how frail our baubles are, what fading phantoms these;
Fat fields and teeming cities and good ships upon the seas.

O Lord, this day we come in shame as stewards of Thy store,
Thy bounty we have hid away, e'en as men did of yore;
In swinish, heedless blindness have we bestowed Thy goods,
Heaping here and starving there in wicked, wanton moods.
O Lord, have mercy on us, who have heard the bitter cry
Of them who, broken by our greed, have called Thy love a lie.

O Lord, what are our harvests; O God, what are our gains
That we should boast of them to Thee who sendest winds and rains?
But if the passing year has brought one custom, law or code,
Which makes for Thy kind justice, Lord, here now, in thine abode,
We thank Thee for this signs that Thou still showest us Thy face,
For that, O Lord, we thank thee — that sure proof of Thy dear grace.

(Emporia Gazette, November 27, 1913)

In the Holidays

'Tis chilly when returns come in,
And you have done your part,
To find that the majority
Gave you the marble heart.

'Tis chilly when you woo a girl
To have a rival win,
And get invited finally
To see her marry him.

But, ah, the coldest thing of all
In this chill month, no doubt,
Is to be told at 5 a.m.
"The fires are all out!"

(Emporia Gazette, January 1, 1898)

———

A Prayer for Thanksgiving
I
Lord God, who moved through man's heart
    To make Thy vision real,
Potter who shapeth with vast art
    The ages on Thy wheel —
Kings, nations, races, pass Thy way,
    Beneath Thy guiding hands;
How do they flick, like wasted clay
    And crumble on the sands!
O God, Thy knife, in blood and strife
    Is molding truth from dust;
Make us more worthy of Thy peace
    Make Thou, our works more just.

II
God, hold from us Thy blade of war,
    Its cruel, useless stress;

Yet we seek only at Thy bar
    The peace of righteousness.
For peace with wrath of class or clan
    For peace that pales with fear,
For peace with wrong twixt man and man
    We do not ask Thee here.
God with Thy dole, purge Thou man's soul
    Of malice, greed and lust;
So lead us in the walks of peace —
    God, make our ways more just.

III

From wars that burn in agony,
    Banked smoldering in hate,
The bound child's moan, the woman's cry
    And man's dumb curse at fate,
From wrongs that foul the people's blood —
    Thou fair and sweet they seem,
God hold us, stay us; turn the flood,
    Choked in the law-dammed stream.
Thou, Jacob's God, spare not Thy rod;
    Smite Thou our heart's proud rust.
Lord, make us worthy of Thy peace —
    Our works and days more just.

IV

O, dreaming Potter infinite,
    Who toileth with the clods,
Who formeth beauty in His might,
    And turneth men to Gods —
May we who writhe this fleeting hour
    Upon Thy wheel in pain —
May we who only know Thy power
    Have faith it is not vain.
Break us, O Lord, upon Thy sword,
    Remake us, as Thou must;
And for that we may serve Thy plan —
    God make our hearts more just.

(Emporia Gazette, November 26, 1914)

Christmas Eve

The time has come for Santa's call!
So close your eyes, my children small,
And don't you dare to peek!

He'll fill your stockings full of toys
Old Santa loves good girls and boys,
He'll steal without the littlest noise
Adown the chimney tall.

Perhaps he'll leave a shiny tree,
With sweets and gifts for you and me
So go to sleep, my darlings wee,
Tomorrow you'll have all.

(Emporia Gazette, December 24, 1926; printed on the newspaper's covering wrapper.)

———————

PHILOSOPHY AND RELIGION

THAT YE BE NOT JUDGED

From a till the gold coin vanished;
  It was stolen; and to-day
From the world the thief is banished —
  Thief's an ugly word to say.
You who never knew of sinning —
  Strong in manhood from your youth;
You who from your life's beginning;
  Never loosened hands with truth —
    Are you the judge?

Yonder walks an erring woman —
  Heartless, hopeless, in the mire;
Painted, brazen, scarcely human
  In her gaudy trade attire.
Passing her, you give no token —
  You of sinless, baby face —
You to whom mere words unspoken
  Are the chains of her disgrace —
    Are you the judge?

He was "murdered," said the jury;
  In the viscid, musty cell
Paces one whose fatal fury
  Did the deed; you said: " 'Tis well" —
You who take life school-girl fashion,
  You who never spat at Fate —
You who never fondled Passion —
  You who never suckled Hate —
    Are you the judge?

They have broken vows like basting;[1]
  They are underneath the ban;[2]
She, her wifehood's portion wasting —
  He, his world-chance as a man.
You whose heart has ne're caught anchor

Deeper than Life's drifting mold;
You who never felt the rancor
Of a duty-love grown cold —
                    Are you the judge?

(Kansas City Journal, January 24, 1892; *Rhymes by Two Friends, 164-65.* • 1. A severe beating. • 2. Below public disapproval or condemnation.)

––––––––

Some Secular Queries

At the corner of my street
        There is one,
Whom I almost daily meet —
        She's a nun.
And for many a long day
I have wanted nerve to say:
"May I walk along your way —
        Little nun?

"With you I'd be glad to chat,
        Little nun,
'Bout the weather and all that —
        Just for fun.
And should you remove your mask,
I would probably ask,
How you like your lonely task,
        Little nun.

"I am curious to know,
        Little nun,
What you think about the row
        You've begun.

Do you ever sit and muse
On the earthly joys you lose?
Do you ever have the blues —
      Little nun?

"I suspect that you are human,
      Little nun;
And my guess is, that as woman
      You've been won.
Does he ever haunt your dreams,
Till his old-time shadow seems
Near you in the noonday dreams,
      Little nun?

"And you love him anyhow,
      Little nun?
Come, be honest with me now,
      We've begun.
Don't you tell me you have not
An unconsecrated spot;
Do not say you have forgot —
      Little nun.

"For the Lord who made your mother,
      Little nun,
Uses one plan and no other
      To work on.
In the corner where you keep
Woman's fancies, don't you peep,
When you think the Lord's asleep,
      Little nun?"

(Kansas City Journal, May 15, 1892; *Rhymes by Two Friends,* 158-60.).

The Facts About the Pharisee

Some nineteen hundred years ago there lived in Galilee
A scholar and a gentleman who was a Pharisee.
He doubtless had some sesterces[1] and ducats[2] in his day,
But sadly lacked somewhat of tact when he went up to pray.
And History, the dealer, wasn't square, you understand,
And didn't give the Pharisee a chance to fill his hand.

And so he stood on deuces, when his flush might have been royal
If History had played the game on rules laid down by Hoyle.[3]
Therefore there's no injustice — (as the Pharisee is gone) —
In running through the pasteboards[4] to see what he might have drawn.
He proudly prayed his ante[5] in; but Hist'ry had him canned:
She didn't give the Pharisee a chance to fill his hand.

He might have been and likely was one of those decent chaps,
Who paid his debts and held aloof from vulgar crowds; perhaps
He didn't see the reason for parading with the lodge;
And may be when they wanted men for Santa Claus he'd dodge;
Perhaps he really wasn't much like other men he scanned,
And History, the dealer, didn't let him fill his hand.

He doubtless didn't prance about from Rome to Jericho,
On various excursions when the highway rates were low,
And when his daughter married off the Pharisee did not
Nail on a brace in market place a list of what she got.
Nor when he put out liquor did he brag about the brand,
But Hist'ry would not let him "stay" nor let him fill his hand.

So let us draw this moral with the forceps of regret:
Don't sit into a poker game above your social set.
Beware of Fame and History who play a game of steal.
Although they bluff, they're safe enough: They always fix the deal.
Consider well this ancient sire whose ruin these two planned —
They didn't give the Pharisee a chance to fill his hand.

(*Kansas City Star,* September 17, 1892. • 1. A Roman coin, originally of silver, later of brass, equal to 1/4 denarius. • 2. A gold coin of several European countries. • 3. Edmond Hoyle (1672-1769), English writer on games. • 4. Colloquial for playing cards. • 5. A card player's stake put into the pool after he sees his hand but not before he draws other cards.)

In the Beginning

When God was aglow with His work on the world,
    That stood on the structure of Faith,
He hewed out the winter and lustily whirled
His hammer aloft, and with fancy unfurled
He dreamed out the summer; then as His lips curled
    In a smile (like a heavenly wraith[1]),
His hands slowly fashioned the smile of His face,
    And wrought there the beautiful thing
Unknown to the Worker who bent o'er the place
Where winter should be — full of joy at the grace
Of His dream; but at least, God beholding the trace
    Of His smile on the world — called it Spring.

(*Rhymes by Two Friends,* 1893, p. 211; also entitled "How It Happened" in manu-
script. • 1. An apparition of a living person in his exact likeness.)

Comfort Scorned of Devils

O let me keep the sorrow in my heart,
    That God has sent, nor hope that it may go;
    O rather let me pray I may not know
The empty day when sorrow shall depart,
And leave me callous with no tears to start,
    When mem'ry trips upon my heart-strings, though
    My soul shall writhe with anguish, — be it so:
Why, only quick hearts quiver 'neath a dart!

For Joy or Love or Sorrow keeps the heart alive,
    And moistens it with Hope, that parching heat
    Of passion may not crust it as a glove.
Then let me live, O God, and ever strive
    To hallow Sorrow; O it is as sweet
    To live for Sorrow as to live for Love.

(*Rhymes by Two Friends,* p. 213)

Elder Twigg's Philosophy

How they comin'? O jest fair —
    — Fair to middlin';
Chuck to eat and duds to wear —
    Uh-m-m fair to middlin'
I'm one them men who never get
Particularly overhet
When good or bad luck comes — and yet
    I'm fair to middlin'.

I figger things run jest about
    From fair to middlin'
First and last, day in, day outs,
    Jest fair to middlin'
You'll find a smile for every tear,
And vicey vercy, never fear;
The world keeps even — pretty near —
    At fair to middlin'.

It's better when you're that a-way —
    Say fair to middlin',
And can keep happy, as I say,
    At fair to middlin',
I claim a man don't have to choose
'Twixt Paradise and the calaboose;
You're jest as fat and lots more use
    At fair to middlin'.

(Kansas City Star, July 15, 1894)

A Reason in Rhyme

A long time ago,
Twenty ages or so,
Before there was any world here,
Our thoughts and our dreams
Were coiled on the beams
Of a sun that had run out of gear.

And all stowed away
Awaiting the day
When men should demand them, they were —
All fancies unused,
All tales unperused,
Star-dusty in primeval blur.

But when God had whirled
This top of a world
A-spinning on infinite space,
Then man gasped in awe,
At the wonders he saw;
He prayed for an undefined grace.

And an angel who heard
That prayer without word,
Uncoiled all our dreams from the skein,[1]
But cut them in strips
For our poor mortal lips
With his flaming sword swinging a-main.[2]

These angel-clipped shreds
Of thought are called words,
And thus does it happen betimes
That the angel will strike
Off two pieces alike,
And these we poor mortals call rhymes.

When the angel made grief,

The next stroke brings belief
And morrow bears sorrow away;
   For those who use sad
   The angel makes glad
And sleeping stills weeping for aye.

And who so hath sighs
The angel makes wise,
For regret doth forget all her wrongs;
   And thus from the heart
   That is bruised cometh art
And sobbing bursts throbbing to song.

Our hearts, O my sweet,
Ran on Heaven-scanned feet
A-weary, my dearie, through time.
   Till thou gladdened me,
   And I told it to thee,
And our souls kissed and quivered in rhyme.

(Kansas City Star, November 30, 1894. • 1. A loose, twisted loop of yarn or thread.
• 2. With great strength and speed.)

The Average Life

The common places seeping through the day
Are drops that fill the goblet which men say
Is sour with sorrow. May not blessings lose
Their sweetest flavor by continued use,
And sorrows, therefore seem more bitter far
By their infrequence than they really are?

When I am done with life let this be writ:
"Life gave him more than he gave back to it.
The tears he shed refined his cup for him,
While joy kept bubbles smiling to the brim."

(Kansas City Star, February 17, 1895. At this time the average life expectancy for
men and women in the United States was about 47 years.)

The Ballad of Mary and Elisabeth

*And Mary abode with her about three
months, and returned to her own home.*

This ballad shall tell of two mothers
 Bearing their quickening young;
What prayers were prayed,
And what blessings were laid,
 What peans and hymns were sung.
Hopes? Yes, such as all mothers must have.
 Faith? Well, so it may be.
But one son's head
To a tyrant was fed;
 The other son died on a tree.

————

And deeply they counselled together,
 These mothers of Jesus and John;
Counselled, aspired and dreamed great dreams,
 The while they were hurrying on;
Hurrying on to the River,
 Where Life goes down to meet Death,
Where Life trembles, falters and rises or falls
 On the turn of a sigh or a breath.
And thus as they sat at their sewing —
 The barren old wife and the maid —
High were their hopes and their yearnings —
 Solemn the vows that they said.

Then all of the griefs and the sorrows
 And all of the woes of their race
And all of the anguish of unspoken shame,
 Their children were destined to face —
Came welling up out of their harts to their lips
 And entered the threads that they plied.
For mothers' hearts hurt at humanity's wrongs,
 Though their hands may be hopelessly tied.

Then Mary, aglow with her passion,
　　The passion that aches for a word,
Lifted her voice in the grief of her heart —
　　Lifted her voice to her Lord.

And all that was mother within her
　　Cried out for the weak and oppressed,
Stung by the thought that the soft little feet
　　Just fluttering under her breast —
Should travel the weary and profitless way
　　That led to the world from her door;
So Mary, carrying Jesus unborn,
　　Sent up her prayer for the poor.

"He hath filled the hungry with good things,
The rich He hath sent away,
He hath scattered the proud in their wickedness;
　　He hath bidden the meek to stay;
He hath put down the mighty from power
　　And to those of low degree
He hath given his blessing of righteousness —
　　He exalteth even me."

So prayed in the house of Elisabeth
　　Our Most Gracious Lady then,
The prayer of world-old motherhood,
　　For peace and good will among men.
The Lord He hath answered Our Lady;
　　He hath taken her son to the cross
And Mary is standing apart from the throng
　　With only her faith for her loss.
But surely and steadily upward
　　The pathway from Mary's low door,
Leads to a better abode in this earth,
　　For the weak and oppressed and the poor;
Leads to the hope of a glorious dawn,
　　Of a better and brighter day;

Leads to a time of abundant life,
    Points to a better way.

O Mary, dear mother of Jesus,
    For all of the prayers you spoke,
For all of the fears and all of the tears,
    And all of the press of the yoke —
The yoke of your heartbreak and anguish,
    That Calvary scarred on you there,
May we who have seen the great answer
    That God has returned to your prayer —
May we have your trust and your courage,
    May we have your infinite hope,
And knowing God's plan must be hidden,
    Hold faith in its infinite scope.

And now to the millions of mothers
    Who sit in Elisabeth's home
And pray the great prayer of Mary,
    God let her great privilege come;
To give to mankind without flinching,
    In field or in mine or on sea,
Flesh of their flesh, bone of their bones
    And heart of their hearts if need be;
To yield all for love and for justice,
    Not counting its cost nor its worth,
But following Mary, of Nazareth —
    Spend all for peace in the earth.

(Emporia Gazette, December 25, 1912)

———

To a Son of Joseph

I

Because you walked with us in earth
    And worked in pain and died,
The stream of life that fed your birth
    Rose to a higher tide;
In bloom and bird and beast and tree,
    In song, in joy, in grace —
You drift with that unfathomed sea
Of earth's strange immortality
    Which breaks on time and space.

II

Because you lived with common men
    And wrought in common clay,
Because you reached our common ken,
    And kept our common way,
Because you flinched at every dart
    That men know — e'en at death —
So now you live a sacred part,
Of man's aspiring common heart,
    Immortal as his breath.

III

But oh, for that you loved — you loved,
    There was your soul unfurled;
There glowed the quenchless torch that proved
    God's signal to the world.
Here life had been; here men had stood,
    Here dauntless faith had prayed;
But only God's own herald could
Bring that undreamed of brotherhood
    Which met death undismayed.

IV

The changeless change of passing things
    The far-wrought spell of mind —
Ashes and fancies — on what wings
    These phantoms ride the wind!
But since our God in gladness willed
    In man His deep desire,
Love's impact through the earth has thrilled,
And you, O Christ, on men have spilled
    Your love's immortal fire.

(Emporia Gazette, December 25, 1915)

The Easter Song of Mary Magdalene

I

My heart is a-throb with a song for you,
    Out here where the skies are wide.
For oh! now I know that you live anew,
For oh, that your promise is true, is true,
My charnelled soul has arisen, too —
    My soul that I thought had died.

II

For you who uncovered my leaden heart,
    Fining its dross and alloy,
For you who smiled at my shameful art,
For you who bade all my devils depart —
Oh you — you are here and my pulses start,
    Dancing in new-found joy!

III

To me — even me — first of all you came!
    (And ah, but the earth is fair!)
And oh, but there burneth a sheer white flame,
Cleansing my heart's red chalice of shame! —
My heart that shall shrine ever one dear name
    For you — you — you are there!

IV

So let me sing where the skies are blue,
    Here where the white petals fall.
Oh, let me dance all my joy for you!
For you have arisen — my dream is true,
And Master, my soul has arisen, too,
    Out of its hateful thrall.

(Emporia Gazette, April 22, 1916)

A Sea Song

At high tide and low tide
    In rough seas or calm
Sings on the shore,
    God's monotonous psalm.

At sunset or moonrise
    By star light or day
The dull foolish breakers
    Drone out their hoarse lay.

Wordless and mystical
    Rhymeless and drear
God's voice through the sons
    Awaited man's ear.

Treeman and stonechipper
    Shepherd and Greek
Each one has listened
    And heard his God speak.

Fool or philosopher
    Lover or king
Has stood on the beach
    And heard his heart sing.

He heard his heart sing
    In the waves cadent roll,
Of the vision he held
    In the core of his soul.

Falling or rising
    Though waves dance or moan
God's delphic trumpet
    Speaks each man alone.

To each land and race
    To all shores and climes
God through his sea songs
    Brings truth to all times.

Gold clouds and pearl surf
    Woke some soul at morn
That spelled out God's signal
    And beauty was born.

Love prayed with Death
    By the rim of the sea;
The pulsing tides brought love
    Immortality.

O cargoes drift in that are
    Precious and odd
But the songs that the waves sing
    Come winging from God.

At high tide and low tide
    In rough seas or calm
Sings on the shore
    God's monotonous psalm.

(Undated. William Allen White Collection. Emporia State University Library.
Printed with permission of Barbara White Walker.)

The Song of John the Victor

I

Three thousand years have wearied by
    Three thousand years and ten
Since Jesus, Son of Mary, walked
    In agony with men.
Two thousand years since Alfred dealt
    The first fair blow to caste
Another thousand years and more
    Since Lincoln strove and passed.
Jew and Roman, serf and earl
    Slave and lash are gone
But still the Coming Day shows just
    The ancient flush of dawn.

Still wages the old, old way in the earth
    The feud of the proud and the meek
That drafts every child on the day of his birth,
    In the lust of the strong for the weak.

II

Our sun and tides are hitched and taught
    To toil at beck and call
To bring the creature comforts
    That supply the needs of all
So poverty no longer whips
    Mankind to work with fear:
The pull of hope for better things
    Throbs through our social gear.

Those olden days of want and wealth
    Seem quaint, detached and far;
As strange as vice and pestilence,
    As mad and vain as war.

But still the quick seeds of injustice are sown
    In the feud of the proud and the meek;
And still the ripe harvest of hatred is grown
    In the best of the strong for the weak.

III

One by one they grew in price
    And each one had his fling
Employer, prince of industry,
    Landlord, boss and king
But always rose God's righteous meek
    From shop and mine and fen
And lo! the proud were broken
    But lo! pride ruled again
For archer, peasant, merchant, serf,
    Worker, slave or priest —
In rising each forgot his God
    And wallowed with the Beast.

So rages the blood of the brute in race —
    Through the feud of the proud and the meek
Binding our souls here in time and space —
    In the lust of the strong for the weak.

IV

With stones and spears and men of war
    And votes and moral force
Each age has won its triumph
    And held progress in her course.
But such is God's great scheme of things,
    Whereby right conquers wrong,
That pride is ever stark and weak
    And justice ever strong.
Although the victor falls in pride
    Each epoch's gain is sure
And ancient rights are fortresses
    That hold Christ's lowly poor.

But deep as the instinct for food or for woman,
    This lust of the strong for the weak
Handicaps progress and keeps the world human —
    The feud of the proud and the meek.

(Undated. William Allen White Collection. Emporia State University Library. Printed with permission of Barbara White Walker.)

The King and the Carpenter

Out of the merciless roar of the street
    Came a proud king one day.
Out of the blare to a holy retreat
    Came the proud king to pray,
And swift ran the sexton on felt-padded feet
    Shutting the vain world away.

"Lord," prayed the king, "I have covered my crown,
    Lord, I have hidden my power.
Lord, only thou in the state and the town
    Knowest where standeth my tower.
Lord, I would serve without fame or renown—
    Lord, hear thy steward this hour."

The saws and the hammers that plied overhead
    Hushed at the sexton's grave nod;
The organ was smothered, the organist fled,
    A workman slipped out with his hod;[1]
Then fell a great silence discreet and well bred
    The while a king dickered with God.

"Lord God, a white plague[2] hath stricken my son,"
    Cried the proud king in his woe.
"Cure for it, Lord, the wide world holdeth none,
    Help me, Lord — where shall I go?
Wise men and savants and doctors have done
    All their poor sciences know."

"Lord, have I mortgages holden in trust,
    Binding the children of men;
Lord, I rule over the just and unjust,
    Counted ten million times ten.
These will I make to bow down in the dust —
    Bow and accept Thee again."

Spake a poor carpenter standing hard by
    — Hand box and apron he bore;
"Sire," quoth the carpenter, "I, even I
    I have a salve for thy sore.
I have a balm for all kings' sons who die
    Plague stricken, foul at the core."

"I have a philtre[3] for all Adam's seed,
    Take it, sire; be of good cheer:
Life from my brothers the fetters of need
    Holding men bounden to fear —
Fear of cold want 'neath the lash of thy greed,
    Let Love heal all hate hath cursed here."

"Knowest thou, sire, whence the pestilence comes?"
    Questioned this carpenter wight.[4]
"Not with their armies and banners and drums
    Canst thou defeat this dread knight;
Out of the slums, sire — thine own vassal slums[5]
    Riseth thy foreman to fight."

"Out of thy greed, sire, and out of thy power
    Stalketh the plague to the prince.
Out of the slime from thy well-hidden tower —
    However fair be its tints.
Under the blows of thine own hand this hour,
    Sire, doth thy dying son wince."

"Give up the coppers thou stealest by stealth
    Taken in usurious rent!
Give up thy lawful though ill-gotten wealth
    Racked from youth broken and spent!
Give up thy gold minted out of the health
    Of maimed women, pallid and bent."

"Sire, give it back not as ransom nor fine;
    Give it back joyously free —

Love coïned in justice to brothers of thine,
    Let them receive it of thee.
Take off the curse of thy toll from the mine,
    The shop and the field and the sea."

"No longer then, shall the slum and the dearth[6]
    Of sun kill with plague and with blight.
Then shall men toil in good will on the earth
    Then shall men walk in the Light.
Then shall men cherish God's love for its worth
    And know how it worketh His might."

Thus spoke the Carpenter there to the king;
    He who had ears and heard not.
Even the sexton's bright eyes saw no thing
    Save the fair tip that he got.
Woe to that church — what real help can it bring
    To men driven mad by their lot.

Penance for pillage, and pillage of pence —
    When will our blind kings take heed?
Why do men hold to an age-long offence,
    Why must Christ's wounds ever bleed?
Why do plagues thrive beyond reason or sense
    How long must the Carpenter plead?

(Undated. William Allen White Collection. Emporia State University Library. Printed with permission of Barbara White Walker. • 1. A wooden tray with handle, carried on the shoulder to carry bricks or mortar. • 2. Tuberculosis of the lungs. • 3. A potion, drug or charm supposed to produce a magical effect. • 4. A courageous person. • 5. Homes of poor, dependent subjects. • 6. Costliness or famine.)

The Riddle

Whether young men hurry, I beckon;
When old men fail, I trip them;
When mothers bring forth young
And nations hear new liberties
In agony and travail,
I, even I, sustain their faith.

In me are sons conceived
In me are liberties visioned;
Without me Jesus would have been
Nothing but a philosopher.
I am the thrill in the bliss of a kid.
I am the power than runs the suns.

* * * * *

When I recall
Your kindness, all
My poor wits go a-flutter.
I cannot write
Nor yet indite
The things my heart would utter.

My fountain pen
Goes crazy; then
Proceeds to halt and stutter.
My type machine
Balks dumb between
A splatter and a sputter.

I'm in a mood
For gratitude
But simply cannot cure 'er.
So lady, make
For mercy's sake
This book my bread and butter.

(Undated. William Allen White Collection. Emporia State University Library. Printed with permission of Barbara White Walker.)

God and the God-Makers

God made a man out of coarse red clay
    Brawny and big of limb.
And the Rain and the Wind and the Sun unkind
    Beat down and tempered him.
Then man made a god of his own coarse clay
    And garnered grim graces there:
From the Sun, hot hate, from the Rain, cold fate
    From the west Wind, mystery,
And his own flesh shrank from his handiwork
    And in this wise[1] worshipped he.

Then God made a man of a finer grain
    Tried in a fiercer fire,
Where Faith and Love and Sorrow strove
    In the flame that consumed Desire.
And this man's god, it was glorified
    Above the affairs of day.
For it healed bruised woes, and united foes
    And took but a Hope for pay.
And this man's Soul grappled his god till death
    And this wise he went to pray.

Now God is moulding another man
    Out of the new world's clay.
With the tools of his trade have his hands been made
    And his brains is God's work today.

And God may toil for ten thousand years
    On the new man's heart, for sooth;[2]
Grinding out Greed, and envy's creed
    And the law of tooth for tooth.
Then the man shall know God's fellowship
    And his eyes shall behold the Truth.

(Undated holograph, signed. William Allen White Collection. Emporia State University Library. Printed with permission of Barbara White Walker. • 1. Way, i.e., the way of being or acting in a certain manner. • 2. Truth, reality.)

MILITARY

THE BLUE AND THE GRAY ON WILLER CRICK

It might a ben in semty-five er mebbe semty-six,
We first held Deckeration Day on Mud and Willer Cricks;
Fer Willer Crick's cemetery was way behind the town
An' up to then they'd scasely ben a single grave go down.
But long there in the winter, Private William Hoskinson
And Cap McBride they up an' died an' got the thing begun;
Then 'bout the last of April what should ol' man Summers do
But leave this vale of tears, an' sail acrost the deep tide, too.

But ol' man Summers wa'n't much loss, you couldn't really say;
He mostly run to fishin' and to putterin' away.
He called hisself a gunsmith but us folks we said it with
The words "son of" appended, also droppin' of the "smith."
They 'd be fer days on fishin' trips, him an' his youngster Bud,
Down near the mouth of Willer er the south fork of the Mud.
We used to talk him over down at the store and we
Jest guessed he was a rebel 'n' if he we'n't he orto be.

But speakin' of the Deckeration day as I begun,
We planned to git some flowers fer McBride and Hoskinson;
An' as we was a talkin' Bud the Summers' boy kim in
An' saw how things was goin' an' he tried real hard to grin.
I see he couldn't come it though, an' hyurd him give a snuff;
But he went off a whistlin' which I knew was jest a bluff.
An' somepin kinder told me by the tremblin' of his jaw,
Bud's heart was nearly breakin' cause he see we'd snubbed his pa.

So on the day appointed they was citizens on foot,
An' some was on a hoss back an' others on a toot.
The Cornet Band was playin' off the ol' "Dead March in Saul,"
The Sunday school in dresses cool was stuck behind 'em all.
But out there in the graveyard now who do you think we found —
There lay thet little Summers' boy upon his father's mound;
He'd got him some sweet willyums, some sheep sor'l an' sparrow grast,
A little bunch of ground peas an' he'd got pegged out at last.

An' Idy she just raised him up so quietly an' said:

"What are you doin', bubby," as she held his sobbin' head.
An' mebbe they wa'n't flowers put on Summerses new grave;
An' mebbe it wa'n't every loyal boy in blue 'at gave.
That was before we knew the piect they call the Blue an' Gray
'Bout cheers and tears one allus hears on Deckeration Day.
But I stand up to tell the rebs ef I bore them bad blood,
'Twas wiped away that very day by Summerses boy Bud.

(*El Dorado Republican,* May 30, 1890.)

———

BUGLE CALLS

I can't git 'em up!
I can't git 'em up!
I can't git up in the morning.
I can't git 'em up,
I can't git 'em up,
I can't git 'em up at all!
The corporal's worse than the sergeant,
The sergeant's worse than the lieutenant,
And the captain's the worst of all!

Go to the stable,
All ye that are able,
And give your horses some corn.
For if you don't do it,
The captain will know it,
And give you the devil
As sure as you're born.

O, where is that cook gone,
Cook gone,
Cook gone,
Where has that cook gone?
Where the aitch is he-e-e?
Twenty years till dinner time,
Dinner time,
Dinner time,
Twenty years till dinner time,
So it seems to me-e-e!

98

Come and git your quinine,[1]
Quinine, quinine, quinine!
Come and git your quinine,
And your pills!

Soupy, soupy, soup —
Without any beans!
An' coffee, coffee —
The meanest ever seen!

(Emporia Gazette, May 17, 1898. • 1. An alkaloid extracted from cinchona bark that
suppresses erythrocytic forms of malarial parasites.)

Captain Jonas Eckdall

"They buried him in his blue soldier's coat." — News item

After his last tired march he slept
   All in his coat of blue;
Threadbare and faded, but fondly kept
   Half a long century through;
While toil broke men, and their women wept,
   And all the world waxed new.

And all the world waxed new and young
   While he grew old and gray;
New tales were told, new songs were sung
   And new was man's vain way;
Still in his closet the blue coat hung,
   One spot where his heart was May.

One spot, one token of royal youth,
   One robe of a crown-ed king,
One wedding garment that turned time's tooth,
   And stayed time's fleeting wing —
That was the magic cloak forsooth,
   Which gave him everything.

99

Gave him everything taken by time:
　　Power and health and renown,
So he was proud in the pride of his prime,
　　Proud in his march through the town;
Proudly he passed in his garb sublime —
　　Proudly he laid him down.

(Emporia Gazette, November 24, 1914. A long-time Emporia resident, Eckdall was co-owner of the Eckdall & McCarty Building.)

War and Peace

When peace was smiling on the land,
　　John Barleycorn says "I
Maintain a market fine and grand
　　For corn and wheat and rye.
For my demands are hale and true,
　　They are not halt or lame.
Without my still what would we do
　　To boost the farmer's game?
Of all the kinds of men who use
　　The farmer's stuff today
Who is so faithful as old Booze?
　　Who stokes more grain away?"

Then war came scowling o'er the land,
　　John Barleycorn says "I
— By hen I do not understand
　　This senseless hue and cry.
I use a little dab of wheat
　　I use a little malt.
But I leave lots of grass to eat;
　　It's time to call a halt."
In times of war, in times of peace
　　He never seems to tire;
His fake statistics never cease,
　　He's just the same old liar.

(Emporia Gazette, April 28, 1917)

The Corporal's Story

A Fellow doesn't hate the Boche, not really hate each Fritz,
    He hates the things the Germans are, and that hate never quits.
At least that's how I came to feel, but some men — let's sit down —
    I knew a bird[1] once, decent guy who came from Hagerstown.
Now this here bird, his name was Hale, wan't hostilely inclined.
He was the average run — no more; just fair and square and kind.

We used to sit around the fire and brag and brag and blow
    About the strafe[2] we'd give the Boche; I guess it's always so.
War makes us that way but we were, not ever really vext.
    We tried to mess up Fritz one hour, and then by hen the next
We fed him cigarettes and gum or beat the lousy scamp
    Out of his helmet, watch or belt, back in the prison camp.

But this here bird named Hale, and him a blushing sergeant, too,
    Was always aching for his chance to show what he could do.
Well, one day, Hale got his chance; all fair and fat and fine.
    When Heine he bobs up one day, alone, out of the line.
Now there was Fritz and up sneaks Hale and smashes Heine blim!
    Hale used his gun-butt, then he turned and jabbed
    the tripes[3] of him.

The Boche he writhes in blood and grime, a kind of dying snake,
    And, crazy, sobbed out "Mutter" like a fellow half awake.
Hale's hands were red, his puttees[4] wet,
    his blouse was smeared and stained,
    The man went dead while Hale looked on with eyes
    and muscles strained,
And there stood Hale all splotched and red;
and there he stood and stared.
    And then upon us boys he turned
    all wild and fierce and scared.

His hands, by God, his bloody hands, before his eyes he held,
    And then he lifted up his face, gazed the sky and yelled,

101

And ran, ran, ran like hell he ran, panting and out of breath,
    Then jumped right into Heine's trench,
    in shame and fear to death!
Hale done it; he sure done just that, you know and I know why:
    The curse of Cain was on his heart — the man just had to die!

And so I say about the Boche — you hate 'em — kind of — yes,
    But only hate the things they are — their stinkin' ornriness!
The point is, Hale he killed a man, a poor prune of a Fritz.
    It wasn't war, but murder, and that was why Hale quits.
I mean, a man don't hate each Fritz, but hates the Boche en massed!
    Our outfit stood for Hale and all he done there — at the last!

(Undated. William Allen White Collection. Emporia State University Library, with
permission of Barbara White Walker. • 1. Synonym for fellow or a guy. • 2. Severe
punishment or heavy automatic gunfire. • 3. Any worthless, offensive person. • 4. A
leather wrapping around the lower legs.)

―――

The Ballad of John Beasley

John Beasley had no lofty dream; he was no theorist.
He ambled slowly to the desk, and said he'd not be missed;
So things being equal, why he might as well enlist.

He learned to be a soldier man, with all his might and main,
Though whether he was pleased or not, was never very plain.
Yet John took what was coming, in the sunshine or the rain.

The night they sent him on a raid, he hemmed and hawed a bit;
And if he was afraid or glad, he never mentioned it.
But when he came back from the job, the Boche[1] knew he'd been hit.

So titled on a box John sat, the day the summons came,
Decrying and explaining the injustice of his fame;
Examining his medal while he hooted at the same.

102

And when the fragment grabbed him, — say — he never winced nor cried;
But gave a puzzled troubled look, amazed and stupefied;
Then kind o' slumped down in his pants, and then he sort o' died.

The angels rose to greet him, but the moment he appeared,
(They knew he was the son of God, all shy ashamed afeered)
And then despite his protest, why they more than half way cheered.

The opal sea at sunset, and the mountain's after-glow,
The wind upon the ripened wheat, the way that lovers go,
The god-like strength of common men, all these are good to know!

(Unpublished typescript, *ca.* 1918, William Allen White Collection. Emporia State
University Library, with permission of Barbara White Walker. • 1. A German.)

———

The American Legion Button

The little bronze button of gold and blue,
They were wearing it gayly in pride.
It's all so shiny and bright and new,
And the world is covered with morning dew,
And life all joyous with scent and hue,
Is calling youth out to ride,
To ride,
On the journey glorified.

The little bronze button of blue and gold
With youth goes riding away.
But life may falter and days grow cold,
When the little bronze button is dim and old,
And all it means is a tale that's told,
To the youth of another day,
Hi hey,
God spare you that other day.

(*Emporia Gazette,* September 23, 1919. The American Legion was founded in Paris
on March 23, 1919.)

The Impatience of Youth

A soldier of the Legion was parading on the dock,
His pants were draped at half-mast and he only wore one sock,
"I left my other leg in France," the broken soldier wailed,
"I gave it for democracy, which rather went and failed.
I also gave it for the war to end all war," he cried,
"And now I'm waiting for a boat to seek the other side.
I want to go to San Mihiel! Oh, take me there I beg,
For someone surely stung me and I'm gonna get my leg!"

(Emporia Gazette, January 30, 1923)

An Intermezzo for the Fourth Act

If my peculiar pulchritude in Paris seemed to please
Upon the Champs Elysées 'mongst the blooming chestnut trees;
Or if along the Rivoli in hell's melange of men
Which bubbled in the war-brew, you observed me now and then;
Or if the picture rising, of my rolly poley form,
A-toddle down the boulevards, should make your heart grow warm —
O Phillys, wipe that picture from your mem'ry cold and flat —
     You should see me in my new straw hat!

For I'm in London now, my dear, in London old and gray,
And spring is fading in the past, and summer's under way.
But London is a decent town, polite and smug and curt.
It breaks her heart to frivol and you break her laws to flirt!
And how she works and how she frets, and yet she's always sweet;
So I am here in London for to give the town a treat.
And if I'm middle-aged and bald and slow and rather fat —
     You should see me in my new straw hat!

Perhaps we're not immortal, lass, but O I wish we were;
Though not to save some prudish saint or pale philosopher,
I want to find those lads whom life's sweet poignant beauty wracked,
Who had to duck and cut the show before the second act —
Say Schubert, Keats or Phidias, those olden golden boys —
And tell them something of the play, and how it never cloys.[1]
For I have seen three acts, and now I'm fifty, but at that —
    You should see me in my new straw hat!

(Franklin Pierce Adams, compiler, *Innocent Merriment; an anthology of light verse.* New York: Whittlesey House, McGraw-Hill, 1942, 470. White sent this poem from London to Adams and Ray S. Baker in Paris for their pressroom's bulletin board; also in: Walter Johnson, *William Allen White's America.* New York: Henry Holt, 1947, 309.
• 1. It never satisfies.)

KANSAS

Kansas — There She Stands

Out of a motionless ocean of sand,
Whose petrified billows stretched far to the west,
Kansas sprang up like an enchanted land,
With wealth more than many a king can command,
Where civilization's first favors expand,
Pork packers, pap, passes and poets on hand —
Who says that our State is not wondrously blessed?

(The Lance, December 20, 1890; *El Dorado Republican,* December 26, 1890;
Supplement to the *El Dorado Republican,* June 5, 1891.)

———

The Kansas Renaissance

There's a notion which is prevalent among the people East,
That the West is all Philistine, or Barbarian, at least:
That our ideas are plebian, our ambitions very low,
And we lack that jenny say pa quah[1] they call finess, you know.
But this state of things is changing: Culture now supplies her wants
At a saylong in Topeky of the Kansas rainysauns.

But this saylong, as they call the move, has not assumed as yet
Such proportions as to give High Five[2] a very grave backset.
For it's really just an effort of a few congenial souls
To withdraw from Dame Society and her extensive tools;
To eschew her midnight lunches and her dizzy, vulgar dance —
Hence the saylong in Topeky of the Kansas rainysauns.

They have bid farewell to Strauss' strains and taken up Daudet;[3]
They have quit the giddy gallop in a cold unfeeling way,
They have left the old Virginia reel, the schottische and Berlin,
And are reading French philosophy and topics close of kin;
And they've undertken Zola[4] — ony sway kee mally pants[5] —
Is the motto in the saylong of the Kansas rainysauns.

(Kansas City Journal, November 3, 1891; • 1. Je ne sais pas quois is French for "I
don't know what"; • 2. A card game, see also "High Five on Willow Creek"; • 3. Alphonse
Daudet (1840-1897), French novelist; • 4. Emile Zola (1840-1902), French novelist; •
5. Honi soit qui mal y pense is French for "Evil to him who thinks evil.")

The Interregnum

Us fellers hev a hundred ways
    To tell the seasons by;
Not countin' in the kind of days
    Ner culler of the sky
Fer them is purty badly mixt
    An' jes as like as not,
'at when you git yerself all fixt
    Fer it to be right hot,
The wind'll kinder siddle 'round
    An' give a sudden whoo,
An' set yer teeth to shakin', an'
    Yer hands to gettin' blue;
But if they's any wether 'at
    You can't depend on't all,
It's when the Kansas summer is
    A turnin' into fall.

They's no use much to write it down
    An' stowe it 'way in books,
Next year perhaps 't'll change aroun'
    In all exceptin' looks
Of trees an' grass an' sich like things
    They's jes one way to tell.
An' that's to watch what each year brings
    An' stay here quite a spell;
An' when yer see the yeller's
    All blowed off the sunflower's head
An' the orn'ry little fellers
    Fightin' with 'em now they're dead;
An' when yer see the blue smoke hang
    'Round woods an' hills an' all
You bet the Kansas summer is
    A turnin' into fall.

An' when yu're loafin' by the creek

Down at the swimmin' hole,
 The lonesomeness jes makes you sick,
  Fer not a single soul
Is in to wet thol' spring-board
  'At seems so warped an' dry;
The slidin'-down-place, too, is rought
  By cattle passin' by.
So when you git to town agin
  They hain't a bit of harm
In stoppin' where the sun hes bin,
  (The sidewalks is so warm)
To rest yer tired foot 'at's got
  A sticker in the ball —
All these're signs 'at summer is
  A turnin' into fall.

An' when we hev to wear our shoes,
  The mornin's 're so cool,
An' when we get a good excuse
  To take 'em off at school
At recess to play "three-ol'-cat,"
  Er "scrub," or "pull-away,"
Er any other games like that
  Which all us fellers play —
It feels jes like the spring wuz here
  To be barefoot again —
But though ar feet seem cold an' queer
  When school is taken in,
With all the girls a snickerin' es
  We stand 'long side the wall;
Us boys we recomember then
  'At summer's turn't to fall.

(F.H. Barrington, *Kansas Day — Containing a Brief History of Kansas.* Topeka, Kansas: George W. Crane, 1892, 184-86.)

A Song for Kansas Day

Wandering children of Kansas away,
    By mountain, by desert or sea.
Feasting or fasting, at prayer or at play —
    Whatever your fortunes may be —
Open the doors of your hearts to the breeze —
    Prairie winds never are still —
Hark to the surf of the cottonwood trees,
    The breakers that bloom on the hill.
Open your soul's windows — let in the sun —
    The prairie sun gay with delight,
Where'er your wandering pathways have run —
    Come home tonight.

Come home where Kansas lies under the stars
    Twinkling back beauty and joy;
Come and let homely love poultice your scars,
    Leave off your restless employ.
Come home where summer winds billow the wheat,
    Where golden tides cover the sands;
Come — let your hearts' longing hasten your feet
    And home unfetter your hands.
Come where the sunflower eagerly bends
    A tawny frank face to the light;
So do our hearts seek the joy of old friends —
    Come home tonight.

(Emporia Gazette, January 30, 1915; January 29, 1925; "Kansas Day," celebrated annually, was inaugurated January 29, 1861. Ironically, White died on "Kansas Day" in 1944.)

Another Good Rain and the Farmers Are Jubilant

I

Oh the corn is on the blink
    And the wheat is full of rust,
The alfalfa's turning pink
    And the creek's about to bust
      Out on the plains.
O the oats is out of sight
    In the water and the beans
Are blown higher'n a kite,
    By the passing submarines,
      And still it rains!

II

Wow! it rains
On the panes —
Pitchforks, razors and chilblains,
Colored infants and remains
Of cats and dogs and aeroplanes!
And it roars
While it pours
As the farmer does his chores,
In diving bells; and bores
Postholes in the atmosphere
To find his gates and doors.

III

O it's grand to be a farmer and to poke 'round in an ark,
To fare forth to feed the chickens in a staunch seaworthy bark;
    Oh it's fine to be a farmer
      And grow goose webs on your feet,
    And to buckle on your armor
      And swim out to cut the wheat.
    O the mermaids in the kafir[1]
      And the seacows in the dell
All are joys that make a salve for

What would otherwise be hell.
And now the drouth is broken let's be joyful in our gains,
Let's kyoodle, whoop and holler for these million-dollar rains!

(Emporia Gazette, June 17, 1915. • 1. Any of certain grain sorghums derived from one species *(Sorghum vulgare),* and cultivated for grain and forage in dry regions.)

The Kansas Spirit Speaks
I
This tale
Of how men fail
And stumbling rise again,
And struggling forward fall,
Only to grow through all
Brave and wise and kindly, then,
To pass through life's strange
Alchemy of death, and change
Armors for another battle of God's war
Upon some other star —
This tale I tell today is told
In pictures mirrored back through time
Unlocked from the past's cold rime.

II
And I
Who standing by,
Have seen all and have made
All that is good and ill
Impartially light and shade,
As I patterned the dreamer's will —
I am the spirit or ghost,
Or genius or troll of these plains,
The weaver who ravels life's skeins,
Or if you like it most
Call me the Goddess of Fate.
For I, only one of the lesser gods,

114

Read what the master dreams!
Refashion this dream; I create
Life, events, destiny out of the clods —
　　Molding them,
　　Holding them,
　　Folding them,
　　Into such figure and scheme
　　As out of the infinite, gleam.

III

Only dull seas
Covered our leas,
Eons ago ere the coming of man,
　　Yet the dreamer dreamed
O'er a world that seemed
Stark, cursed, mad, without purpose or plan.
　　Then came the prairie grass
　　　Then rose the wind
　　　　Then from a cloud
God let His signal pass
　　Into a mind!
　　　　Then a head bowed.
Idols came, orgies came, blood came, and fire.
Still rose man's frightened face, higher and higher.
　　When came the love of gold,
　　　Then man touched hands,
　　　Hunted in bands,
　　　And out of far lands
　　Came eager searchers bold,
How gold love dragged them
　　'Neath the hot sun!
How famine fagged them
All back but one —

IV

One May
There came a day
When men rode on these plains and hills
　　Hating and fighting and burning their souls;

115

Slaking the thirst that kills
With malice that seared them like coals.
Then out of the depths of the mud
    In the black muck of mad hearts,
        War blossomed red.
And I, even I drew the blood,
    I fashioned their hell-blooming arts,
        I checkered my woof[1] with the dead.
And man said God was asleep,
    And crouched before Moloch[2] or Baal,[3]
When slowly, from out of the deep
    I saw all the blood blossoms pale,
And fruit of the fruitage of peace.
Yea, out of these hideous loams,
Out of the hate-dregs and lees
    Rose love — fair love and its homes.
For evil, wrong, error and sin
    That trap, leash, handcuff or pain
Man in the midst of life's thrall
    Are hurdles that help us to win.
Win through the strength that we gain.
    Whether we clear them or fall
    For though we lose at Time's goal,
    Yet we know life in this earth
    Reaches its highest worth
        Not in the cheap
        Gold counters we keep
        Nor in the crops we reap;
But in the growth of soul.
Thus evil in God's will
Is good disguised as ill.

V

    And so
    The pictures go.
Here sorrow is pied[4] with joy,
    And there is what seems like a break
        In the web itself; but no, see
The figure which seems to annoy

As a fragment — observe your mistake? —
Is only the plan spreading free.
Here comes a vast, crazy joke,
A prank of some harlequin brain;
But lo, 'twas the dreamer who spoke
Through a fool in the Lord's high disdain —
Disdain for the pride of the wise,
In love for the weak who could rise
In score for the thews[5] of the strong
In love for one cursed by the throng.
So God dreams each epoch its lot.
And here in this strip called a state
Good men or bad times or not
The picture designed here by fate
Seen small or peered at from the marge
Blights faith, stings hope, mildews love;
But prayed over, viewed from above,
There God's scroll is written in large.

(Topeka Capital, November 10, 1915; Kansas State Teachers College, *Teaching,* II (November 1, 1915), 10-13. Partially reprinted in *Literary Digest* (New York), LII (January 29, 1916), 240. Celebrating the 50th anniversary of the Kansas State Normal School in Emporia, this poem views the pageant of Kansas history, the church missions, pioneer life, territorial government, the Civil War, grasshoppers and the drouth. • 1. The threads that cross the warp in a woven cloth or texture. • 2. A semitic deity, whose worship was accompanied by human sacrifice — especially of first-born children. • 3. A Semitic name of several ancient deities, in general worshipped for soil fertility and increased flocks. • 4. Colors in blotches, piebald or variegated. • 5. Muscular power, strength.)

Labor Omnia Vincet[1]

The hot winds are here but what do we keer?
And why should the farmer have fits, poor thing?
His corn is secure but he is blamed sure,
It won't bring him more than two bits, poor thing!

(Undated. University of Kansas, Spencer Research Library. • 1. *Labor omnia vincet,* labor conquers all.))

The Kansas Boys

If you grew up in Boston and have played in Faneuil Hall,
You likely won't appreciate the following at all,
For though 'tis said that Kansas is the child of Plymouth rock,
You can't say she takes after her prim Puritanic stock.
She isn't much on culture and is rather scarce on "aht:"
The crop of May theosophy is also very short.
But if you're after comradeship with its peculiar joys,
Just pack your grip and take a trip to Kansas with the boys.

Then stop off at Topeka; hunt up Jim and Jake and Tell;
They'll show you thro' the state house and the Santa Fe as well;
You'll shake hands with the governor and have a little chat;
They'll steer you to Ben Simpson, of the supreme bench. If that
Does not fill you with glory, and the senate chamber fails,
They'll take you to the club room where the royal Elk regales.
There's a beaux esprit and jeu d'esprit and sprees with romp and noise:
Over in Topeka, on a visit with the boys.

At Lawrence they will show you up Mount Oread of course;
And then Learnard will take you out to see his pacing horse;
At Wichita they'll take you up into the Eagle roost,
And tell you of the furniture and how the people used
To have to keep an automatic register to say
The price a lot would sell for at a given time of day.
They'll tell you of the paupers who one day were fortune's toys,
Out at the Peerless Princes, out in Kansas with the boys.

And when you're in Emporia, don't leave the town till you're
A friend of Colonel Whitley and have seen his famous sewer.
Then spend a day in Atchison and look up Charley Styles,
And let him take you to the club and smother you with "smiles."
And when you climb up to the gate and when you faintly rap,
Don't ask him if your soul may go to reap eternal joys,
But tell him that you've pegged a seat among the Kansas boys.

(Undated. University of Kansas, Spencer Library.)

NEWSPAPERDOM

Some Shop Talk

When the office is deserted in the evening, and your cares
Have trooped off with the devil as he shuffles down the stairs,
When you pace about your kingdom like a chained and restless pup,
And walk back to view the galley rack to see how much is up —
Before you go to supper, put your tired brain to soak,
And try to wash the kinks out with a quiet little smoke.
    For it's smoke, smoke, smoke,
    Makes the world seem like a joke;
        With its shirling,
           Curling,
              Swirling,
When there's nothing that is sterling,
After all its strange unfurling
    Only smoke,
    Purling smoke.

Sit and laugh at "Old Subscriber" and the papers marked "refused."
Take a puff at the Alliance[1] that imagines it's abused.
Smile in triumph at your banker and the man who holds your note;
O'er your master, that old "plaster," gloat a tranquil, haughty gloat.
And as evening shadows thicken, pull your seed until it beams;
Such sweet sunshine out of sadness in a cloud of silver dreams.
    Oh, it's dreams, dreams, dreams;
    Life is only what it seems;
        And like mazy,
           Dim and lazy
Shifting cloud-forms weird and crazy,
Our distinctions are; so hazy,
        Motes and beams —
        Only dreams.

(Kansas City Journal, November 7, 1891; *Rhymes by Two Friends,* 184-85. • 1. The Farmers' Alliance, organized in Kansas in 1890.)

A Print Shop Incident

An old typographical error —
One of the old-fashioned school —
    With the old-fashioned stagger,
    The stoop-shouldered swagger,
Sat there on the rickety stool.
He'd "hoofed it clean in from Salina."
He said, with a make-believe cheer;
    But there rasped in his throat
    A corn-husky note,
'Twas truly pathetic to hear.

So over we went to the Red Light
To let the Rum Fiend do its worst;
    For an image of wood
    Most assuredly could
Not withstand such an eloquent thirst.
Some wandering Corsican minstrels
By the door played their plankety plinks;
    He heeded them not,
    But sped to the spot
Where Cholly was doling the drinks.

Perhaps you have seen an ecstatic
Delirious bliss in the face
    Of a man who's in love,
    As he prances above
The low earthly joys of his race;
Perhaps you've seen pictures of halos
O'er transported features of saints;
    Or looked when she smiled
    In her sleep at a child
For whom heaven's own artist paints.

Well, if you've seen such an expression
You've an idea then, like as not,
    How his face lighted up

As he dropped the tin cup
When the liquor got down to the spot.
He rolled his eyes wistfully doorward;
With his hand wiped the liquor away,
And said in a low,
Quiet voice: "Let us go
Out an' hear them 'ere eyetalics play."

The standard of morals was low then,
Before the descent of St. John;
And a man got his rank
From the size of his tank,
And the number of drinks he had on.
And so when I dream of a heaven,
I think of a place where they say:
"That's the stuff; ain't it though?
Now come on an' lets go
Out an' hear them dang eyetalics play."

(Kansas City Journal, December 8, 1891; *Rhymes by Two Friends,* 181-83; *Kansas Newspaper World* (Hiawatha, Kansas), I {October 1894}, 3.)

———

Where "A Lovely Time Was Had"

Bill Hucks,[1] the item-chaser on the *Willer Creek Gayzette,*
Was the likeliest hustler that old man McCray could get.
As a writer-up of runaways, an' funerals, an' shows,
Bill never had an equal, nor a rival, goodness knows.
So we sent him up a invite to a doin's Susie give,
And he writ a piece about it that was fine, as sure's you live.
But all I kin remember is, "We hardly need to add
The guests agreed at leaving that a lovely time was had."

O, yes — come now to think of it — her maw cooked up some cake,
And pies and floatin' island truck that Susie helped to make.
And they was pickle-lilly, too, and beets and jell and jam,
And slaw, and chicken salad, and some sanwiches of ham.

And them Bill said was "viands," which, in writin'-up he owned
"Made a tempting feast of good things, and the table fairly groaned.
And when the wee sma' hours were come, we hardly need to add,
The guests agreed at leaving that a lovely time was had."

Old Bill has gone from Willer Crick; the *Gayzette* is no more;
For Old McCray has stole away to find the Golden Shore.
And Susie has been married off for lo! these many years,
And some of them that come that night have quit this vale of tears;
But maw has in her scrap-book — 'long with little Laury's death,
And the pome about the baby and the accident to Seth —
The piece about the doin's, and today it makes us glad,
To read at Susie's party "that a lovely time was had."

(*Kansas City Star,* September 21, 1892; *Rhymes by Two Friends* {1893}, 169-71;
Emporia Gazette, October 15, 1895; *The Kings and Queens of the Range* {Kansas
City, Mo.}, October 15, 1897, 195; *Sunflowers; a Book of Kansas Poems* {1916}, 36-
37. • 1. Although there was a Colonel William "Bill" Hucks of the Upper Slate
Creek in Center Township, Kansas, who was elected as a delegate to the State
Republican League convention in Topeka, White here uses both Bill Hucks and the
Willer Creek Gayzette as pseudonyms with no reference to Colonel "Bill." See also,
" 'Col. Hucks' on Col. Harris.")

"Twinkle, Twinkle, Little Star [1]
How I Wonder What You Are."

How I wonder if I may
Hitch my cart to you to stay.
How I wonder if there be
In you some divinity.
How I often fear your glow
Soon will flicker, fade and go.
How I fear each passing cloud
Lest it wrap you in a shroud.
How I love your little light,
How I hope to keep you bright.
Yet I feel, Dear Star, if you
Dim and darken in the blue,
That my deadened soul will know

Something of an after glow,
And will life be — though unlit —
Sweeter than you shone in it.

"Twinkle, twinkle, little star,
How I wonder what you are."

(*Rhymes by Two Friends,* see *recto* of unnumbered page preceding p. 153. • 1. Soon after it began publishing in 1880, the *Kansas City Star* became known colloquially as "The Little Twinkler." Here, White expresses his appreciation for the opportunity to work for this newspaper.)

——

Old Slug Nine[1]

Old Slug Nine quit work today,
Old Slug Nine is dead they say;
Summers, autumns, winters, springs,
Have flown by on silent wings
All unmarked, save by the click
Of the seconds in his stick,[2]
Since he went with boyish pride,
To the alley where he died.
There he wore his life away,
Old Slug Nine is dead, they say.

Old Slug Nine quit work today,
Old Slug Nine, bent, grim and gray;
Yet there was a time when he
Listened to the Prophecy
Youth spake from the land of dreams —
Smiled and listened — while the themes
Of a thousand anthems pealed
In a heart where Promise kneeled;
And yet, grim and bent and gray,
Old Slug Nine quit work today.

Old Slug Nine quit work today —
All unknown, yet who shall say
That in his unhonored lot,

Plodding humbly, there was not
All the joy and happiness
Found in fickle Fame's caress.

Had he bartered for a place
In the mad, soul-killing race,
Giving up his simple joys,
Twinkling eyes and kindly voice —
Would our throats choke, as we say,
Old Slug Nine quit work today?

Old Slug Nine has come today,
To the end of his lone way.
Would that favored lives when spent,
Taught such sweetness and content —
Taught that peace is not the crown
Of the king or claquing[3] clown;
Calloused hearts are never glad,
Richly eased or poorly clad.
One glad heart is still today,
Old Slug Nine is dead they say.

Old Slug Nine quit work today,
Old Slug Nine is dead they say;
Summers, autumns, winters, springs,
Will flit by on noiseless wings,
All unmarked now by the click
Of the seconds in his stick.
Yet he lives, and death's undone,
If there be so much as one
Lonely soul sob when they say,
Old Slug Nine quit work today.

(*Proceedings* of the Second Annual Meeting, Kansas Editorial Association, convened at Hutchinson {Kansas}, Monday and Tuesday, January 22 and 23, 1894. Sterling, Junkin and Steele, 1894, 20-21. "Passing of Slug Nine" was dedicated to Talbot Childers, Emporia printer, and read to the Association meeting, January 22, 1894. Also published in the *Kansas City Star,* January 29, 1894. • 1. This nickname referred to a strip of metal, smaller than the height of type, to space between lines of set type. • 2. A composing stick in which type was set or arranged. • 3. A paid applauder at a play or speech.)

The Late Alex Butts[1]

Life's day, however dreary,
  Comes, some time, to its close,
And then the toiler weary
  Lies down to his repose;
Lies down at last forgetting
The staring and the sweating,
The planning and the fretting
  That every toiler knows.

The irksome bonds that bound him
  Like broken fetters fell:
His comrades gather round him
  When sounds the solemn knell;
They use no hollow phrases;
They roam no wordy mazes;
But give this best of praises;
  "He did his work so well."

(Emporia Gazette, March 7, 1910. • 1. Alexander Butts, the senior editorial writer
for the *Kansas City Star,* was a Republican in his 60s in 1893. Butts wrote "Kansas
Notes" in the *Star* for many years.)

Obituary

Alas, no more the shooting stick[1] will click against the quads;[2] nor
will the forms be justified by little paper wads; no more will old
subscriber sigh, and constant reader moan; no more, alas, will type-
lice gaily scamper o'er the stone. For they have locked the office and
the ghost no longer walks; and there has come a silence in the place
where money talks. Today there smiles a specter with a haggard
mein and gaunt, where yesterday there blossomed forth a little
Long-Felt Want. And, O, they let it languish, and O they let it die,
and gave it neither sustenance, nor patronage, nor pie.[3] And still
they gave it sympathy, and yet they gave it cheer, and now they
stand a mournful group, and sob around its bier. And see the wet-
eyed mourners heave their aching liver pads, who let their darling
perish for the want of proper "ads." For it had little job-work and

subscribers but a few; but O, it had bright prospects and its skies were ever blue. But prospects would not pay the hands, nor blue sky pay the rent, and so the Long Felt Want[4] hiked up into the firmament. And now it rests in glory; it has left us sobbing here, while those who watched it wane away may drop a silent tear.

(Emporia Gazette, January 12, 1911. • 1. A hand-held composing stick used to set or arrange type. • 2. A block of type metal lower than the body having a type-face of letters, used in spacing blank lines. • 3. Mixed or disarranged type. • 4. The Long Felt Want referred to the *Gazette's* dwindling economic condition and White's almost desperate attempt to rebuild its subscription and advertising operations in the face of rising labor and equipment costs.)

Some Thoughts on This Occasion

There's a rumble in the distance and a sizzling in the air;
There is language in the atmosphere and sulphur everywhere.
The cow is on the bookcase, the pinanny's on a chair!
    See that wagon load of verses and a clothes rack and some souse,[1]
    Well, it's Uncle Walt[2] a-movin' to his
                Brand
                    New
                        House!

Oh, the cat is in the cupboard, the canary's in the cat;
The phonograph is pickled in a tub of anti-fat,
While the Haviland[3] and hardware are stamped down neat and flat,
    O, the things that he's a thinking but not saying to his spouse
    While Uncle Walt's a-movin' to his
                Grand
                    New
                        House!

So let us stuff the cotton of forgiveness in our ears,
And may the Angel Steno,[4] blot her record with her tears;
But let us all rise up and give our fellow cit[5] three cheers!
    For he's a good old Injun, though he's modest as a mouse —
    Which Uncle Walt is movin' to his
                Fine
                    New
                        House!

(Emporia Gazette, December 10, 1914. • 1. Something soaked in pickle juice, like pigs' feet. • 2. Walt Mason (1862-1939); White hired him in 1907 to be a news reporter and editorial writer. • 3. Fine china porcelain dishes. • 4. The office stenographer — without whom no newspaper could have survived. • 5. Citizen.)

Shorty [1]

My stock of heroes never wuz
So very big, you see, becuz
I never understood the plan
'at they are built on, an' a man
Don't like to keep things 'round that he
Can't predicate, at least that's me
All over an' that's why, you know,
I got to liking Shorty so.

He wa'n't no hero, Shorty wa'n't,
Jes' a ornery tall slim gaunt
Ol' print 'at loaft around the den
An' read exchanges,[2] working when
Some print upstairs 'u'd want to quit
An' take a lay off from his sit.
He wa'n't so awful extra though
At stickin' type — a little slow
Perhaps because he wuzn't pat
At soljerin' the hook fer phat.

And pore? Well, now, you're talkin' right;
He was the dernest looking sight
Regarding clothes you ever saw;
Last year's bird nest wouldn't draw
Wu'th a cent 'gin Shorty's show.
Shorty's wife was diff'rent though:
Jes' as different from him,
Plump and short as he was slim.
Brisk and lively, too, I guess,
Yet I bet the lovinges'
Girl you find in any state —
Shorty thought so't any rate:

129

"My ol' woman," Shorty'd say,
In a lovin', tender way,
'at 'u'd do a man more good
Than a dozen sermons would.

Shorty never paid to go
To any circus, fair or show,
He just 'u'd show his rule[3] and smile,
Wink and walk in slick as ile.[4]
An' so I bet when Shorty dies
An' hits the road for Paradise
His golden rule'll pass him through
Jes' like his other used to do.

(Undated; William Allen White Library. Emporia State University. Reprinted with permission of Barbara White Walker. White may have written this while employed by the *El Dorado Republican*. • 1. Shorty's surname may have been Bates. See also "Shorty Bates" in "A Twelfth Month Idyl." • 2. Exchanges were newspapers sent free to other newspapers to provide news — especially of local interest. • 3. A thin plate of metal, usually brass, the height of ordinary type, with a line or lines as its face. • 4. An adjectival suffix signifying *suited for* or *capable of.*)

Oh, For Uncle Walt

A cruel war has come again to haunt our peaceful dreams; to flash the sword and sheathe the pen, while ravaged freedom screams. A thousand, thousand strategists beneath our starry flag are fighting, bleeding, dying, as they masticate the rag. Oh, who will sing their battle hymn and twang their lyres of praise? Oh, who will croon the doleful tune, the dirges and the lays, to crown those heroes on the stools who bear the battle's brunt, on the Coca-Cola sector of the drugstore front?

Oh, come, Walt Mason, drop your lyre in blissful praise, and join the chanting, yodeling choir to celebrate them guys. See how they sit in serried ranks across our lovely land, a bloody crew at G.H.Q. who gripe to beat the band. Oh, Uncle Walt, sing an assault — some sobbing lyric stunt — upon the coke offensive at the drugstore front!

(Emporia Gazette, May 17, 1940; a "machine poem")

THE DREAM CATCHER

*Beautiful as the Sentiment
that surrounds them*

Climatic Evolution

A changing of the seasons is evident to all;
The coolness of the summer and the hotness of the fall.
The snows of June and August and the blizzards of July,
Bring a longing for December and its atmospheric fry.

Busy workmen tread the river in the chilly month of May,
Cutting blocks of frozen crystal for November's sweltering day;
While the snows of June come swirling from dark, overladen skies,
Feed the streams that roar and rumble in the February rise.

As the May days feebly stagger to the open arms of June,
And the frozen earth gives answer to the leafless branches' tune,
Comes a longing for the odor of the newly slaughtered hay,
When the January mowers get in their deadly play.

(Kansas City Journal, May 24, 1892)

———

A July Idyl

One summer night, with pensive thought,
    I sat within my chamber door;
Anon an insect hum I caught,
    And soon I heard a dozen more.
They sung and sung, I know not what —
    "Comrades," perhaps — some awful bore;
They sung and stung, I fiercely fought —
    No use, they bit me o'er and o'er.
All night they on my carcass wrought
    And waded deep into my gore;
In vain I peaceful slumber sought,
    All night I rolled and tossed and swore.
Some pennyroyal oil I bought
    Next day, and rubbed in every pore.
With insect oaths the air's now fraught —
    I calmly sleep and snore and snore.

(Kansas City Journal, July 16, 1892)

A Rhyme of the Dream-maker Man

Down near the end of a wandering lane,
    That runs 'round the cares of a day,
Where Conscience and Memory meet and explain
    Their quaint little quarrels away.
A misty air-castle sits back in the dusk
    Where brownies and hobgoblins dwell
        And this is the home
        Of a busy old gnome
    Who is making up dream-things to sell,
        My dear,
    The daintiest dreams to sell.

He makes golden dreams of wicked men's sighs.
    He weaves on the thread of a hope
The ariest fancies of pretty brown eyes,
    And patterns his work with a trope.[1]
The breath of a rose and the blush of a wish
    Boiled down to the ghost of a bliss,
        He wraps in a smile
        Every once in a while,
    And calls it the dream of a kiss,
        Dear heart,
    The dream of an unborn kiss.

Last night when I walked thro' the portals of sleep
    And came to the weird little den,
I looked in the place where the elf-man should keep
    A dream that I buy now and then.
'Tis only the sweet happy dream of a day —
    Yet one that I wish may come true —
        But I learned from the elf
        That you'd been there yourself
    And he'd given my dear dream to you,
        Sweetheart,
    He'd given our dream to you.

(*Kansas City Star,* September 14, 1892; *Rhymes by Two Friends* {1893}, 166-68; *Club Member,* VII No. 7 {March 1909}, 6; J.H. Powers, ed., *Some Emporia Verse* {1910}; *Poems that live forever,* selected by Hazel Felleman. Garden City, N.Y.: Doubleday, 1965, 94-95. • 1. A figure of speech; the use of a word in a figurative sense.)

A Gray Day

Cloudy skies and low —
Not a wind to go
Whispering to the yellow woods
All that winds may know.
Here a berry drops,
There a leaf hangs still;
Melancholy gathers slowly
Over bolt and hill.

While the darkening day
Deepens duskier gray,
Stealthy shadows softly steal
Down the woodland way;
Feeble flowers, unwept,
Fade along the field,
With the mystery of their history
Perished, unrevealed.

If we two to-night,
In the certain light,
Meet, touch hands — half-shadowy
Each to other's sight —
Sudden thrill may loose
Lips from silence' thrall,
Sweetest vision find fruition,
Love be all in all!

(Undated, from "Collected Poems of William Allen White," manuscript compiled by
Donald S. Pady, August 1962, in Spencer Library, University of Kansas.)

WOMEN

TO CHLOE

Now is the day approaching that the poet longs to see;
When "sunny hours" with "greenwood bowers" and "fragrant flowers"
    there be;
When rhymes come at his bidding, without using "know" or "too,"
When "lowing herds" and "loving words" and "cooing birds" are due.
When "the woods are sweet with perfume," when "the languid breezes sigh,"
When "bonny lass" and "waving grass" and "sheeny bass" are nigh.
This is the poet's season and the climax doth appear,
When Chloe reads her essay to "kind friends and teachers dear."

Yon lutist pipes the praises of the maidens as they come:
"To Duty" and "To Beauty" with her tutti frutti[1] gum.
This lyrist times his meter "to the sorceress whose art"
With "her passion" "tiger fashion" claws a gash in Phyllis'[2] heart.
There are those who sing of Psyche[3] and her mild peculiar grace —
In that flighty Grecian nighty, with that highty tighty face.
But I'm still true to Chloe in her graduating gear —
Who flushes o'er the footlights with "kind friends and teachers dear."

Long years ago I loved her and she told me "I love you;"
With the fleetest and completest, sweetest kiss I ever knew;
The mem'ry of that tender look in those coy hazel eyes,
When she'd spoken, is a token of my broken paradise.
A man is given one such chance to mingle with the gods;
If he takes it not, but shakes it, then he makes it with the clods.
And so I twang a cheerful lyre, and dry the trembling tear,
And bet on other Chloes with "kind friends and teachers dear."

(*Kansas City Star,* March 13, 1892; *Rhymes by Two Friends,* 175-77, entitled, "To
Chloe at Springtide." • 1. Candy consisting of different kinds of preserved fruits. •
2. A pretty, rustic girl like Phyllis in Vergil's *Eclogues.* • 3. A beautiful princess of
whom Venus became jealous.)

An Exposition Idyl

Above the pigs and poultry and the crepe and calico,
Above the gaudy tinsel of the pretty passing show,
Beyond the crook-necked squashes dear to ev'ry homely heart,
There is within the darkened room that's set aside for art
A picture of a lady fair, with sweet and tender face,
A picture crowned with golden hair; yet in this quiet grace
Of her blue eyes there surely lies a fearful mental tussle —
For the day dream in the picture wears a bustle.[1]

Oh, say not that the sentient[2] thing of canvas does not feel
The meaning winks and brutal thrusts that coarse men rudely deal!
Oh, say not that the yearning look her eyes so well express
Is for an absent lover and not for another dress!
Oh, think you that the little heart whose flutt'ring glows her cheek
Is timed to some unuttered name her lips dare not to speak?
Not so that blush, that nervous hush, that almost quivering muscle:
The day dream in the picture wears a bustle.

The day was when she wore it with great joy and girlish pride,
When he was billed to take her for their Sunday buggy ride.
Her little brother teased her some, and piled things on it then,
But Jim said it "became her" and her mother smiled Amen.
And wear it? Well, a tug of war would not have pulled it down;
She was the best dressed "people" in the little country town.
But that sweet day has passed away, nor leaves one parting rustle —
While the day dream in the picture wears a bustle.

(*Kansas City Star,* October 5, 1892. • 1. A pad or framework formerly worn under a woman's skirt below the back of the waist. • 2. Capable of sensation or consciousness.)

A Rickety Rhyme of Ye Olden Time

Whylom ther ben a witteless Curl,
    He wont in Olden Tymes;
And eke ther ben a Giddie Girl,
    And he at hire Heort did hurl,
As Wyghtes have done thro alle the Worl',
    So tellen Olden Rhymes.

Sche grette thys Curl with down-cast eyes,
    Lik Maydes of Olden Tymes;
I nolde say whens sche get Hire Syghes,
    Nor gif sche seemed hire Glad Surprise:
No boke canne say whenne woman lyes —
    Not even Olden Rhymes.

He tok thys Sweteheort to ye Schowe —
    Ye pley of Olden Tymes;
They sate hem in ye Choyseste Rowe
    For he hys super wolde forgoe
That he at Nyght myght seme to throw
    On Dogge; so say ye Rhymes.

But whenne Trew Love thys Curl did make —
    Thys Curl of Olden Tymes —
Sche lysten softly whyl he spake,
(I gesse sche wot hys Purs ben brake),
Fr O! sche gave him an Hard Schake,
    So tellen Olden Rhymes.

So full of Sorewe ben hys Cuppe —
    Thys Curl of Olden Tymes —
He tramp-ed alle ye Dayseys uppe
Benethe hire Casement, and ye Puppe
Coude not hys Serenayding stoppe;
    He made thes Cadent Rhymes:

"You came dere, last Nyght in a Raydiaunt Dreme'
And ye Day yt ys ful of your Perfume yet —
— Fragraunt with you, and so Swete doth yt seme,
That God moste have sprinkled from yesterday's Streme,
   (Where our Lyves ran together unchoked by Regret),
A Chalyce of Water that lay in ye Gleme
Of your eyes o'er my Heort, and a myst from ye Dreme
   Fills alle ye Day with your Perfume yet."

Not whenne thys Wyght hys Whyskers grew —
   This Wyght of Olden Tyme —
He got a Wyf as Wyse Men do,
   And lyed about hys First Love Trewe —
— Which schowes he wot a Thing or Two:
   So tellen Olden Rhymes,
            Betymes,
               So tellen Rymes.

(Kansas City Star, October 19, 1892; *Rhymes by Two Friends, 197-99.* White's humorous attempt at Middle and Early English strains the modern readers' interpretations of his tale.)

142

The Old Story on Willer Crick

Miss Ann Elizy Free had taught the school on Willer crick
Sence Nohy turned the cattle out, an' never whipped a lick.
She was one of them fat and jolly sympathizun' souls
The Lord turns out fer mothers, then has slips an' breaks the mol's.
The men folks fer'em's made in: so Miss Elizy grew
To be the foster mother of the whole dern measley crew;
The only human weakness that she never could fergive
Was spoonun'[1], 'an her scorn at that went through her like a sieve.
"Well, mebbe fools is folks, but then," says Ann Elizy Free,
"They haint a bit like other folks is; No! Sir! Ee!"

Of course they used to tease her, but she called a spade a spade,
An' laffed an' said: "Oh, yes: I am a poor dried up old maid."
(She weighed a hundred-forty an' had money out to loan,
An' mebbe that is why the Elder seeked her fer his own.)
But be that as it may, they was no foolishness in theirs —
No lallygaggun'[2] on the stoop, new coo-un' on the stairs.
To meetun' an' to Sabbath school an' sociables they went;
But no unseemly tenderness between the two was spent.
"Fer mebbe fools is folks, but then," says Ann Elizy Free,
"They haint a bit like other folks is; No! Sir! Ee!"

But after they was married you had orto seen the show;
The Elder called her "Birdie" an' she called the Elder, "Joe."
She had him wearun' linen shirts and neckties on week days,
An' breshed his clo'es an' spruced him up a hundred different ways;
She smoothed his hair in company an' fretted an' took on,
As if he was a baby when the little man was gone.
The women ribbed her fer it; but she flared up an' says, "You?
You married folks is heathens; you jest don' know how to do.
Well, mebbe fools is folks, but then," Elizy says, says she,
"They haint a bit like other folks is; No! Sir! Ee!"

(*Kansas City Star,* January 3, 1893. • 1. To act with silly fondness. • 2. This derives
from the intransitive verb, to loll — to move or recline in a lax, lazy or indolent
manner. • 3. Whispering "sweet nothings.")

A Serenade

I fling my kisses at the moon,
  Oh, lady sweet, my lady,
And in its light these rhymes I croon,
  Oh, lady sweet, my lady.
For that, mayhap, some thought of thine
May turn to me, and thy dark eyne
Seek in the moon these gifts of mine, —
  Oh, lady sweet, my lady.

The moon doth make wan lovers bold
  Oh, lady sweet, my lady.
For love is young as time is old,
  Oh, lady sweet, my lady.
E'en as I make these rhymes to thee,
The moon hath lent a grace to me —
Some heart-sore lover's legacy, —
  Oh, lady sweet, my lady.

Dark hours may come and sweet hours go,
  Oh, lady sweet, my lady.
For hours bring joy and hours bring woe,
  Oh, lady sweet, my lady.
But ask the moon in that dread time
For one sweet echo of this rhyme,
And I have wrought a verse sublime —
  Oh, lady sweet, my lady.

(Kansas City Star, March 15, 1894.)

The Maiden and the Prince

There's a half-forgotten story or the echo of a song,
That is tangled in the meshes of my mem'ry, and a throng
Of knights in jeweled armor pass in dignified parade,
Across my fitful fancy, while, upon a palisade,
A wraith[1] of regal radiance illumes the legend fair;
Of the maid behind the trellis and the prince who kissed her hair.

There's a glitter and a glamour in the telling of the tale,
And a golden thread of love is wrapt around the rugged mail,
Till its silky strands seem stronger than the woof[2] of love we know,
As it shimmers in the sunshine on the hills of long ago.
And so lovers of these latter days look back with mute despair
At the maid behind the trellis and the prince who kissed her hair.

Yet the lily lady's lover was a roisterer who fought
Many brutal bloody battles for the booty that they brought;
And his heart benumbed and callous, seared with passion could not feel
The perfumed breath of Love through Hope's enchanted chambers steal.
'Twas the halo of some poet's love that lit the fabled pair:
The maid behind the trellis, and the prince who kissed her hair.

(*Rhymes by Two Friends,* 209-10; *Kansas City Star,* March 22, 1894. • 1. An apparition of a living person in his/her exact likeness, thought to be seen usually just before his/her death. • 2. The threads that cross the warp in a woven fabric.)

The Formal Announcement

That Mister Sims, who's comed out here
To see our Jen for 'bout a year,
W'y yesterday walked in the store
Whur he has never been before.
Yes-sir an' you'd ist orto saw
The way he talked polite to pa.
An' 'en they both looked, in the face,
Zif they'd been 'vited to say grace,
'N' druther not; ist like the mens
We boarded durin' conference.
At last pa ups an' says it was
All right, whatever Jennie does.

That night at supper pa says: "Jen,
I seen that Sims to-day," an' 'en
She doused the lasses on her mush —
Jen did — an' says: "Now, pa, you hush."
An' pa an' ma laffed fit to kill,
An' ast Jen when she thinks she will.
So, when they sent me off to bed,
I heard ol' Mister Simsy said:
"W'y, Jen, you'll break your daddy's chair,"
But Jen she whispers, "I don't care.
We got another; but," says she,
"You needn't tell the fambilee."

(*Rhymes by Two Friends,* 200-201; *Kansas City Star,* November 11, 1894.)

My Lady Greensleeves

Alas! my love, you do me wrong,
    To cast me off discourteously,
And I have loved you so long,
    Delighting in your company.

      For oh, Greensleeves was all my joy!
      And oh, Greensleeves was my delight,
      And oh, Greensleeves was my heart of gold!
      And who but my lady Greensleeves!

I bought the kerchers[1] to thy head,
    That were wrought fine and gallantly;
I kept thee both at board and bed,
    Which cost my purse well favoredly.

I bought thee petticoats of the best,
    The cloth so fine as might be;
I give thee jewels for thy chest;
    And all this cost I spent on thee.

Thy smock of silk, both fair and white,
    With gold embroidered gorgeously,
They petticoat of sendal[2] right;
    And these I bought thee gladly.

Greensleeves, now farewell! adieu!
    God I pray to prosper thee!
For I am still thy lover true:
    Come once again and love me!

      For oh, Greensleeves was all my joy!
      And oh, Greensleeves was my delight,
      And oh, Greensleeves was my heart of gold!
      And who but my lady Greensleeves!

(Kansas City Star, February 20, 1895. • 1. Kerchief, a cloth worn by women as a covering for the head. • 2. A thin silk fabric used in the Middle Ages.)

Hannah Binding Shoes

Poor lone Hannah
Sitting at the window binding shoes;
   Faded, wrinkled,
Sitting, stitching in a mournful muse;
Bright-eyed beauty once was she
When the bloom was on the tree,
   Spring and winter
Hannah's at the window binding shoes.

'Tis November —
Now no tear her wasted cheek bedews
   From Newfoundland
Not a sail returning will she lose;
Whispering hoarsely, "Fisherman,
Have you — have you heard of Ben?"
   Old with watching,
Hannah's at the window binding shoes.

Still her dim eyes silently
Chase the white sails o'er the sea,
   Hopeful, faithful
Hannah's at the window binding shoes.

("Old slugs," *Newspaper West* II, July 1895, 93-94)

The Rhyme of Mignonette

When dandelions fleck the green,
    And plum-blooms scent the evening breeze,
    And robin's songs throb through the trees;
And when the year is raw thirteen,
    And Spring's a gawky hoyden yet,
The season mirrors in its mien
    And in its tom-boy etiquette,
    Maid Mignonette, My Mignonette.

When bare-feet lisp along the path,
    And boys and jays go whistling by,
    And girls and thrushes coyly cry
Their fine joys through the aftermath —
    Then laid ghosts know their amulet
Which fickle siren mem'ry hath;
    So laughing comes that sad coquette,
    Comes Mignonette — my Mignonette.

The wild rose is a conjurer,
    It charms the heavy years away,
    Unshoes my feet and bids them stray
O'er playgrouns where our temples were.
    To some pale star I owe a debt
For harboring the soul of her
    With whom I learned love's alphabet —
    With Mignonette, My Mignonette.

(The Court of Boyville, 1902, 106)

Love's Pleading

O come my love, the jitney[1]
    Waits; the nickel's in
My purse. My sparker snaps at all the
    Fates, for better or
For worse. Let's jit in joy while life
    Is June; five coppers pays
The bill. So come and jitney 'neath
    The moon, along the low grade
Hill. While all the world is smooth
    As glass, while all our tires are
Spry, there's bliss in every quart
    Of gas; let's hit life on
The high. So come and be my jitney
    Queen; a nick is all my
Hoard. Who cares for grief or
    Gasoline? Come mount
My trusty Ford.

(Emporia Gazette, February 16, 1915. "Jitneurs" were those that drove jitneys, which were gas-driven buses operated by the street-car company).

The Super Sex

O mama glanced at papa and she didn't like his hat, and the way he tied his necktie made him look a trifle fat. And she didn't like his haircut and she didn't like his shoes, and the way he butchered pronouns often gave poor mom the blues. So she kind of got to thinking that she didn't care for pa, and being rather pretty mama didn't mind the law. Then mama got the hatchet and some poison and a gun, and also got an alibi and had all kinds of fun. And papa when they found him was a sad an gloomy wreck; with strychnine in his liver and a blow-out in his neck. And the jury looked at mama and she busted down and cried, and the co-respondent took the stand and beautifully lied. And did they send poor mama up to serve her 40 years? No, the jury rose and kissed her, and then handed her three cheers.

(Emporia Gazette, June 24, 1921. White here refers to the famous Kaber trial in Cleveland, Ohio.)

150

The Lady Special

The helpful hen, the milkful cow, the hamful and the pigful sow,
tomorrow will be here to show the farmers how they all can grow,
when treated kindly and with care, and fed on clean and
wholesome fare. The farmer and his kids and wife are asked to
leave their daily strife with wind and wether, drouth and rain, to
see this festive female train. It's free to all, for none can pay. You'll
find it at the Santa Fe. So pack your family in the bus and come,
and have this show on us. You'll learn to beat the farmer game —
you'll be darned thankful that you came.

(Emporia Gazette, May 11, 1922.)

———

All Sorts of Girls

There's the pretty girl,
And the witty girl,
And the girl that bangs her hair;
The girl that a flirt
And the girl that is pert
And the girl with a baby stare.

There's the dowdy girl,
And the rowdy girl,
And the girl that is always late;
There's the girl of style,
And the girl of wile,
And the girl with the mincing gait.

There's the tender girl,
And the slender girl,
And the girl that says her prayers;
There's the haughty girl,

And the naughty girl,
And the girl that puts on airs.

There's the tolu[1] girl,
And the "fool you" girl,
And the girl that bets on races;
There's the candy girl,
And the dandy girl,
And the girl that has two faces.

There's the well-bred girl,
And the well-read girl,
And the girl with a sense of duty;
There's the dainty girl,
And the "fainty" girl,
And the girl that has no beauty.

There's the lazy girl,
And the "daisy" girl,
And the girl that's a merry joker;
There's the girl that's shy,
And the girl that's fly,[2]
And the girl that bluffs at poker.

There are many others,
O, men and brothers,
Then are named in this narration;
There are girls and girls,
And they're all of them pearls,
They are the best thing in creation.

("Collected Poems of William Allen White," *MSS.* compiled by Donald S. Pady, August 1962, in Spencer Library, University of Kansas. • 1. Balsam of Tolu is an aromatic substance from certain plants; hence a "perfumed" girl. • 2. American slang for "knowing," keen or nimble.)

A Santa Fe Incident'

It was silent in the chair car and the clanking of the rails
Made a frame to hang a poem on of jingling joys or wails;
The cattleman from Burlington was drumming on the pane;
The state house clerk was whistling on a card some low refrain;
The high-browed girl from Lawrence was engaged in her "Bazar,"[1]
Der krosry man von Veechita was chewing a seegar,
When the train stopped at Eudora with a fizzle sizzle chug,
And took a soft-eyed siren on the Santa Fe plug.

Her carriage, face and figure were perfection, and her smile
Was a shimmered tangled day dream as she drifted down the aisle.
The cattleman's eyes watered and the state house clerk was dazed;
Der krosry man from Veechita in dizzy rapture gazed;
The frizless girl from Lawrence put her glasses on and saw
A particularly interesting view across the Kaw,[2]
While the siren sat there coyly as a kitten on a rug —
The siren from Eudora on a Santa Fe plug.

And as the train neared Argentine, the cattleman grew rash,
He cleared his throat and nervously pulled at his roan[3] mustache.
Der Veechita man lost his nerve; the state house clerk grew gray,
And as he saw the cattleman he made a bold sashay.[4]
And when at last the train had stopped she answered loud and clear:
"Ay haf a yob av verk oop at des Coates house;[5] call oop dere.
Ay tank Ay lak to sey you more becourse Ay lak you mug."
Said the siren from Eudora on the Santa Fe plug.

(Undated; William Allen White Collection. Emporia State University Library, with permission of Barbara White Walker. In 1886, El Dorado was served by the St. Louis, Ft. Scott & Wichita Rail Road, the Florence, El Dorado & Walnut Valley Rail Road (a Santa Fe branch line), and the Ellsworth, McPherson, Newton and South Eastern Rail Road. By 1893 the Great Rock Island and Pacific Railway connected various Kansas towns as Atchison, Leavenworth, Horton, Topeka, Hutchinson, McFarland, Herington, Marion, Wichita and Caldwell. A northern branch line passed through McPherson, Salina and Abilene. • 1. A fashion magazine. • 2. An eastern Kansas river. • 3. A red or brown moustache. • 4. To walk mincingly. • 5. A fashionable Kansas City hotel.)

Ida M. Tarbell

To I.M.T.
(on looking
at her
portrait)
Oh I have
saw the
Jungfrau
and once I
seen a bust, of
Jove a-frowning
at mankind —
More terrible than
just. Oh I have
cited Jeffries' and
Jim Corbett's fear-
some mugs; and
glimpsed Pike's Peak
and Roosevelt and all the
other pugs. And I have blinked
in wonder at the Mona Lisa's
smile; and once I gawked
at Venus, late of Milo
for a while. But oh I never seen such grim,
peculiar
sphinx-like grace, in all of
them as Ider M. wear
in her fighting face.

(Undated, courtesy Librarian, Ida Tarbell Collection, Pelletier Library, Allegheny College, Meadville, Pennsylvania.)

The Huskin' Bee

The huskin' bee wuz over, ez the sun wuz goin' down
In a yaller blaze o' glory jist behind the maples brown,
The gals wuz gittin' ready 'n the boys wuz standin' by,
To hitch on whar they wanted to, or know the reason why.

Of all the gals what set aroun' the pile of corn thet day,
A-twistin' off the rustlin' husks ez if 'twas only play,
The peartest one of all the lot — 'n they was putty too —
Wuz Zury Hess, whose laffin' eyes cud look you through and
    through.

Now it happened little Zury found a red ear in the pile,
Afore we finished huskin', 'n ye orter seen her smile;
Fur, o' coorse, she held the priverlege, ef she wud only dare,
To choose the feller she liked best 'n kiss him then 'n there.

My! how we puckered up our lips 'n tried to look our best,
Each feller wished he'd be the one picked out from all the rest;
'Til Zury, after hangin' back a leetle spell or so,
Got up 'n walked right over to the last one in the row.

She jist reached down 'n teched her lips onto the ol' white head
O' Peter Sims, who's eighty year ef he's a day, 'tis said;
She looked so sweet ol' Peter tho't an angel cum to say
As how his harp wuz ready in the o'tarnal day.

Mad? Wall, I should say I wuz; 'n I tol' her goin' hum
As how the way she slightes me hed made me sorter glum,
'N that I didn't think she'd shake me right afore the crowd —
I wuzn't gointer stand it — 'n I said so pretty loud.

Then Zury drapped her laffin' eyes 'n whispered to me low,
"I didn't kiss ye 'fore the crowd — 'cause — 'cause I love ye so,
'N I thought ye wudn't mind it ef I kissed ol' Pete instead,
Because the grave is closin' jist above his pore ol' head."

Well — wimmin's ways is queer, sometimes, and we don't allus know
Jist what's a-throbbin' in their hearts when they act thus 'n so —
All I know is that when I bid good night to Zury Hess,
I loved her more 'n ever, 'n I'll never love her less.

(Undated, from "Collected Poems of William Allen White," manuscript compiled by
Donald S. Pady, August 1962, in Spencer Library, University of Kansas.)

ORDINARY PEOPLE

CONCERNING THE GRIPPE[1]

There's many a different way you can find
To tell if this trouble afflicting mankind,
This new influenza that's driving men blind,
    Is working your friend who has sought it;
The good, plain, old-fashioned, American way
Is to come up behind him and friskily lay
Your hand on his back and cheerfully say
    "Ah there old Feller! You got it?"

Or you can approach him without any fear
While eating his wienerwurst, switzer and bier,
Kleine pretzels he munches while drinking his beer
    And wipes off the "bead" from his lip.
Wen sie sprechen and sagen to him as you pass[2]
"Guten abend" und so weiter — Vell how you vas?[3]
He'll say in reply o'er his foaming brown glass:
    "Wie gebt es bei innen und hast du die grip?"[4]

You'd better proceed in a different way,
    And put on an accent quite furrin and flip;
You'd better blow low and throw in just a few
Unaccented vowels and consonants too
And say: "Je suis glad I have met up with vous;
    Mais avez vous, mon cher, la grippe?"[5]

(El Dorado Republican, January 17, 1890; Health concerns forced social barriers especially when contagion separated sick and healthy. By 1900 the five leading causes of death were: Pneumonia and influenza, tuberculosis, diarrhea, heart disease and stroke. • 1. "La grippe," or the grip, meant influenza. • 2. When you speak and say to him as you pass. • 3. "Good evening" and so forth — Well, how goes it? • 4. "How goes it with you and have you the grip?" • 5. "I am glad I have met up with you; but have you, my friend, the grip?")

The Old, Old Story

It was on a still June evening (as all proper tales begin),
When day had left the east bars down, and let the night troop in,
And all the eight crop not tramped up at twelve or thereabouts
Was one large patch of moonshine, and some stubble star grass sprouts,
This of course is not unusual, and has happened oft before;
But 'tis meant to be poetical like J. Philander Moore.
    O, it's J. Philander Moore.
Was purveyor of dried codfish in his father's grocery store.
    But his tastes and things were higher,
    And he therefore did aspire
    To acquire by his lyre,
    Love and glory; while his sire,
    In the mackerel clothes — pin mire,
                  Only swore.

J. Philander loved Lucinda Smith, as "man ne'er loved a maid."
So this fair night, the same fair knight, a serenade essayed.
He practiced "In the Gloaming" and "Susanner Don't Yor Cry,"
And "O Come Where the Lilies Bloom," and "Emmet's Lullabye."
He wasn't much on Schubert, and on Abt was only fair:
But his favorite for every night was "Rahzers in De Air!"[1]
    "O De Rahzers in De Air."
Is a little "colored" ditty that will tend to curl your hair.
    "Come 'round some udder night,
    "Foh dees boun' tuh be a fight:"
    Runs this light and almost trite
    Anacreontic aerolite;
    "There'll be rahzers" — gleaming white —
                  "In De Air."

Lucinda's great aunt, deceased upon the Smoky Ben,
Was brought home for interment and she lay in state there when,
Philander twanged his sweet guitar: Lucinda in a fright,
In sotto voice through curtains said: "Come 'round some other night."
Wherefore the song bird started up his much loved "Rahzer tune,"
And bayed full fifteen stanzas to the giddy, giddy moon.

Oh the giddy, giddy moon,
Ducks behind her white cloud apron when she sees young lovers spoon.
    But alas, Philander Moore!
    All his spooning days are o'er,
    In the store, sick and sore,
    He sprouts Peach Blows[2] on the floor;
    For his one, first, last amour,

                Passed with June.

(El Dorado Republican, March 13, 1891. • 1. "Rahzers a-flying through the air" was a popular vocal song, often sung by KU's Arion Quartet; see also, "Apollo on Willer Crick." • 2. A glaze of a delicate purplish-pink color like peach blooms.)

Concerning the "Old Crowd"

By Colonel Hucks[1] — with due apology to Mr. Riley[2]

I ben to our convention at Topeky, an' I see
The way the thing was goun, an' it kinder saddened me.
Not 'at it ain't as loyal an' as rousin' as of old;
Not 'at the speechifyin' wan't rantankerous an' bold.
Them young bucks done ther duty an' they shoved the old thing
        through,
An' they got along as smoothly as we ever used to do —
But they was somethin' lackun, somethin' missun from the day —
I want to see the old gang stay.

Of course it hain't the fashion fer to grieve an' take on so
About them good old timers thet a feller used to know.
My heart is cracked an' thirstun fer the old time crowd again —
I want to take the kiver off an' let the joy rain in.
I want to hear ol' Hammy speak — what has become of Lew?
I want to hear Jim Hallowell, an' Barney Kelly, too;
These young high tender fellers may be all right in their way —
I want to have the old gang stay.

I used to set an' lissun, an' let loose all bolts[3] an' soar
Till my heart 'ud be a flut'rin' like the old flag, an' the roar

Of the guns at Chattanooga an' of Gettysburg came back,
An' mem'ry 'ud be gropun 'long an old grass-covered track.
I didn't hear the argument, an' didn't seem to keer,
But when the speaker'd rest his voice, I knew 'twas time to cheer.
An' so I want to hear them onct agin, an' so I say —
I want to see the old gang stay.

The good Lord knows we labored hard to give the old state birth;
The good Lord knows our time is brief for stayin' here on earth;
At ev'ry single meetun we are five or six men short,
An' soon they'll have to call us the minority report.
I don't say as your shevun, boys, ner pushun more'n you ought;
I guess you love the loyal men with whom yer daddies fought;
But I'm so kinder lonesome here, and childish like — and say —
I want to see the old gang stay.

(*Kansas City Journal,* March 6, 1892. • 1. White's occasional pseudonym. • 2. James
Whitcomb Riley (1849-1916), American poet, whose style White emulated. • 3. To
blurt out.)

Briggs at the Country Hotel

C. Algernon Briggs, who has been on the road,
    Since last May, is fully aware
That social distinction's all stacked in one load,
    For his frail young shoulders to bear.
This worries him some, you can see by his brow,
    Where breaking's begun before fall,
By that grim old specter that handles the plow,
    And furrows the foreheads of all.
C. Algernon's line is imported cigars,
    As one would infer from the swell
And the boisterous fuss he makes on the bus
    — When Briggs strikes the country hotel.

The porter is "Cholly"; he calls the clerk "Joe,"
    Says: "How are they comin' now, Jim?"

While rolling his name on the register so
    That even the boarders know him.
"You'll give me the bridal room, eh? Joey, dear,
    And Cholly, you take up my case —
And say, Cholly, bring me a bottle of beer
    From Old Billy Whittington's place."
At supper it's "Sadie, go bring me a steak,"
    Or "get me an egg, won't you, Nell?"
Or "a lemon, please, Blanche," for he's running the ranch
    — Is Briggs at the country hotel.

At dinner the guests read the bill of fare through
    Save Briggs, who says softly to Dot:
"Just bring me my dinner, now Dottie, won't you?"
    And Briggs gets the best of the lot.
He's free with his money and runs a great bluff:
    "Oh, well, I'll charge this to the house,"
But when he's in town, he's quiet enough,
    And funds it back meek as a mouse.
For there the gay Algernon sleeps in a flat,
    And feeds at a chophouse as well.
Though he isn't deuce high when at home, he can fly
    When he stops at the country hotel.

If I were an artist and wanted the face
    Of Caesar returning to Rome,
Or of Alexander in search of a place
    Unconquered on all the earth's dome;
Or were I a sculptor and anxious to mold
    Proud Cato with haughty lip curled;
Or hew out a figure of Atlas of old,
    Who reeled 'neath the weight of a world —
I'd not copy from the conventional forms
    That all antiquarians sell,
For the whole classic lot, I'd take a snap shot
    At Briggs in the country hotel.

(*Kansas City Journal,* July 30, 1892.)

The Philanthropist

A pleasure 'tis to leave behind
    The city's heat and din,
And hurry to the country side
    When the picnic sports begin.

I tread with deep enjoyment rare
    The woods and meadows green
And view with philosophic mind
    The wonders of the scene.

I love to hear the peanutman
    Extol his fresh roast wares,
And tho 'tis days since they felt the fire
    No doubt my bosom shares.

I love to watch the merry-go-round
    And list its dulcet strains,
And oftimes join in orbic whirl
    The rustic belles and swains.

The popcorn man, too, has a place
    Within my heart of hearts,
And the vendor of the lemonade red
    Can win me with his arts.

I love them all, these fluent men,
    Whose glib tongues oft beguile
A nickel from my slender purse,
    I ill could spare the while.

(Kansas City Journal, August 1, 1892)

Their Poor Daddy

If daddy had plenty of money, my dear,
    My! what a good daddy he'd be.
He'd buy ev'rything in the world purty near
    To give sister Murry and me.
He'd git us the crick fer to wade in, 'y jings,
    And down by the ford where it ripples and sings,
He'd strain out the sunshine and song, and make things
    To play with, fer Murry and me.
      — My, what a good daddy he'd be,
      And he'd buy us the trees
      If Murry would tease —
If daddy had plenty of money.

If daddy had plenty of money, I bet,
    He'd be the best daddy on earth.
They wouldn't be anything we couldn't get,
    No matter how much it was worth.
To play circus under he'd git us the sky —
To make beads for Murry, the stars upon high —
To have pillow fights with, the clouds that blow by —
    No matter how much they was worth —
    He'd be the best daddy on earth.
      Why he'd buy us the moon
      For a toy balloon —
If daddy had plenty of money.

If daddy hain't got any money, I guess,
    He wouldn't sell Murry and me.
We're tow-headed skeezickses, that's what he says,
    And scalawags, that's what we be.
An' n'en when the Riddles ride by in their rig
    'Ithout any children, ol' daddy feels big,
And tells ma he won't fer a farm and a pig
    Swap off sister Murry and me —
    We're skeesickses, that's what we be.
      But Murry, and me
      Are his fortune, says he —
If daddy hain't got any money.

(Kansas City Star, September 30, 1892; *Rhymes by Two Friends,* 195-96; J.H. Powers, *Some Emporia Verse* {1910}.)

A Ballad of the Bottoms

I been a workin' now a year down in the Cypress yards,
An, hain't been gettin' rosy none, ner foolin' wid de cards.
I'd lend de boys a quarter an' I blows myself fer beer,
An' t'ought I was dat solid dat I never could get queer.
So when de foreman jacks me up, I smashed his face fer fun,
Den dances on de carpet, an' a course I gets de run.
But say, you orto seen de gang — dey quits me every bloke;
Dey don' know you from a rabbit w'en your dead flat broke.
        O it's Chonnie how's yer liver,
        An' it's Chonnie how's your hide,
An' it's Chonnie wrap your vest around a glass o' Foley's pride,
Yes, it's Chonnie yer a loo loo wid a seltzer on the side,
— We don' know yer from a rabbit w'en yer busted.

I used to have some people an' dey lived in Riverview,
An' say, but I was in it — well, I guess I was a few.
De'ire daddy ran a crap game an' he dressed 'em fit to kill;
But my it would a rasped[1] you ef you had to pay the bill.
When Chonnie held his job down, w'y his people used to say,
Dat Chonnie was de only mug w'at had de right o' way.
De udder night I goes around — dere sits dat farmer Moak;
Dey don' know yer from a rabbit w'en yer dead flat broke.
        Fer it's Chonnie lemme smood yer hair,
        An' pat yer mussy tie,
O Chonnie dear, our love fer you, will never, never die;
O it's kitchy, kitchy, tootsey while we wink de udder eye —
We don' know yer from a rabbit w'en yer busted.

(*Kansas City Star,* January 27, 1893. • 1. Irritated.)

The Exodus of Elder Twiggs

I been here in the city now since last Thanksgiving day,
A savin' steps fer Nelly — chorin' like as you might say;
A-dubbin' 'round fer David and a putterin' about,
A-takin' care of little Bill when him an' her goes out.
A-course I've had my pastimes an' the things that I admire,
Like watchin' people movin' safes an' runnin' to a fire,
An' talkin' to the milkman — singin' "Buckle Up My Shoe"
Fer little Bill to laff at like his mother used to do.
But 'en my other daughter's writ fer me to come agin —
So I guess I'll go to Julia when the spring sets in.

They hain't no settled weather much till after March I know;
I want to be on deck,[1] though, as the sayin' used to go.
I want to be on hand the day the younguns rake the yard,
An' the night they have thur bonfire; an' when Julia rends her lard.
I want to cut the fat fer her, an' if they kill a shoat,[2]
To get a little fresh spring meat, I want to have a vote
In givin' Budd the fixins an' the tail to little Net;
An' someone's left the stone off of the pickle pork I bet.
The brine must need a change by now — to let it spoil's a sin —
So I guess I'll go to Julia when the spring sets in.

I want to be around the day they take the peach blows[3] out,
An he'p Budd sort 'em over an' to find the longest sprout.
I want to scrape a apple jest uncovered from the ground
Fer Julia's youngest baby, while the ol' familiar sound
Of stirrin' up the buckwheat cakes the hour of bedtime tells,
An' soothes the heart to rest jes' like a chime of home-made bells.
I want to see the children in thur nighties like a swarm
Of little home-made angels bring thur pillows down to warm.
I want to taste ol' home-made joy and home-made love of kin —
So I guess I'll go to Julia when the spring sets in.

I think 'at when the weather limbers up and easies down,
I'd like it say some Sunday fer to jes' sneak through the town,

167

An' rack⁴ out for the timber, takin' little Budd along
An' him an' me smoke grapevine an' pertend they's nothin' wrong;
An' stretch out in the sunshine on the gravel by the crick
A-knowin' meetin's going' on — not carin', though, a lick;
A-gettin' loads of red buds an' sweet-will-yums an' (b'gosh)
A mess of greens to boil fer Monday's dinner when they wash!
* * * * *
This boughten jam of joy is spread on city life too thin;
So I guess I'll go to Julia when the spring sets in.

(Kansas City Star, March 20, 1893; *Rhymes by Two Friends,* 219-22. • 1. An allusion to baseball's "on-deck" circle, where the game's next batter warms up. • 2. A young hog. • 3. A glaze of a delicate purplish-pink color, applied especially to a Chinese porcelain. • 4. A horse's gait.)

"A Very Present Help"

If you were ever called upon to stand before a crowd —
If you have ever seen your courage wobble as you bowed —
If you have ever felt yourself the mark for gloating glee
That audiences like to prod their victims with, then we
May sing a loud hosanna such as only martyrs can
To the jolly little lady and the big fat man.

O who can see her sympathetic smile and fail to feel
A throbbing wave of gratitude across his innards steal?
O who can hear his hearty laugh and hear him thump the floor
And not desire to be his willing slave forever more?
O where is panting vanity that does not love to scan
The jolly little lady and the big fat man?

O the man who yawns and stretches and the man who snaps his watch
Are around to stretch your temper to the very highest notch;
There's the woman with the noisy boy that toddles in the aisle
And asks his mother if it won't be over after while.

But sun spots do not dim the world, nor shade the shining plan
Of the jolly little lady and the big fat man.

So here's a song of thankfulness upwelling till it chokes
My slender piping little voice to those who see my jokes;
To those whose eyes see tender lines, and glisten in a fog,
And don't glare at "your humble" like two bumps upon a log.
Of all such now on earth there are no better samples than
The jolly little lady and the big fat man.

(Kansas City Star, April 8, 1893)

The Case of Mr. McWhorter

McWhorter was a poet and he parcelled out his past
In rondeaus, songs and serenades of supersoulful cast,
And he sold the same for sesterces[1] wherewith he broke his fast.

McWhorter told the tender tale to maidens by the score
And every time he told it he got hints for three or four
Particularly pleasing poems worth a "V" or more.

McWhorter heard with pale alarm love's shrill seductive fife;
He yielded but his Muse remained the mistress of his life,
So he lived a year in clover sapping sonnets from his wife.

McWhorter found his babies paid him more than ought beside;
He turned a tuneful lullaby when any of them cried —
And he cleared three hundred dollars on the little boy that died.

McWhorter grew luxurious and proud and ran in debt,
And sought to sing of penury and meet his payments, yet
The interest ran faster than his halting pen — you bet.

169

McWhorter faced the music though and tried to pay his note,
(He'd pumped his old-time fountains drier than a last year's moat)
So in mercenary shamelessness above is what he wrote.

The moral of this tearful tale for him who runs to read
Is: In the line of poetry no rich man may succeed;
For no one but a hungry man will slash his veins and bleed.

(Kansas City Star, June 20, 1893. White disliked poetic drivel contributed to
newspapers, especially funeral verse. • 1. Ancient Roman coin.)

Welcome! Sir Knights

Here at this Ancient Landmark where errant Knights have trod,
Where men in joy have labored in the trust and fear of God,
We welcome you as brothers who have passed beneath the rod.

For ye have groaned in bondage, ye have striven with the beast
That grapples man to make the world a bloody carnal feast,
Yet, have ye conquered Greed and Lust and faced toward the East.

And here to you in this man's town a welcome kind we bear
For we are kindred in one brood of toil and moil and care:
Ye have met us the Level and we greet you on the Square.

(Emporia Gazette, May 9, 1911. Five hundred Knights Templar (York Rite Masons)
attended the 42nd annual Kansas Conclave in Emporia.)

The Grand Old Man

I am a grand old man!
Sometimes I feel like a smooth-faced boy
In the earliest spring of his youthful joy,
As I merrily frisk and skip apace,
And paw up the clover around third base;
Stop balls that never were stopped before,
Eat up base hits and clamor for more;
Dash hither and thither in quest of flies,
And gather in whatever comes from the skies;
And line it to first so straight and true
That its wake has a beautiful yellowish hue.
And in critical moments I swing my bat,
And trouble ensues, take a tip on that;
So true is my eye, my arm so free,
That the deadliest pitcher is pie for me.
Now anxious and troubled the baseman stands,
As I kick up my heels and clap my hands;
And away, I am off like a frightened deer,
While the shouts on the bleaching boards[1] I hear,
Sweeter than note of Aeolian harp,
"Well! Well! Well! What's the matter with Carp!"
And I laugh to myself, for that, you see,
Is the kind of a grand old man to be.

And then again!
There comes a day when my muscles relax,
When I'm full of scrap iron, nails and tacks,
As I stand on third like one that's glued
To a proper and dignified attitude;
And I spurn the ball as it ambles by,
And I scorn the bait of the tempting fly,
And I juggle the grounders and throw to first
In a style acknowledged to be my worst.
I stand at the bat with shaking nerve,
And I savagely bite at the wide out-curve.
On the coaching lines I forget the tricks

171

That I mastered in 1776;
While on from the bleachers comes the shout,
"Go hire Jim Davis and let Carp out!"
Ah, those are the times when it comes to me
How wretched a grand old man can be!

But let that pass!
For praised be the gods I am still on earth,
And have safely weathered my second birth;
And I know full well, come smiles, come frowns,
That a grand old man has his ups and downs.

(No publisher listed, but printed poem has date of 1891 handwritten above title.
William Allen White Library, Emporia State University. Published with permission
of Barbara White Walker. • 1. Bleachers; stadium or baseball park seats around the
"diamond.")

————————

The Social Triangle

A slippery, shimmering milk-colored sea
    Too sleepy and lazy to sigh,
Purrs on the beach like a cat on your knee
    All under a hazy lead sky.

Three men of us stand out dark, sombre and brown,
    Not counting the lady in red.
There's Joe whom I knew as a boy in the Town
    And me and the gink[1] on ahead.

Joe lives like a prince at the summer hotel
    Supporting a racing machine
He wouldn't know me from a rabbit — so, well
    I pass up old Joe and his queen.

The gink, he is out in his boat by the kelp[2]
    Lifting his nets from below

Working along with the world's hired help
    For me and the lady and Joe.

Me? I am sprawling and lolling about
    With life rather weary and drab,
Now and then clawing a round pebble out,
    And hitting the ocean a dab.

Fame surely has strung us high on her line —
    There's Joe with his world-famous pranks
And me with my name carved and whittled so fine
    On hundreds of depots and tanks.

We left school along in the eighties and went
    Meandering down the broad grade,
Examining things each one after his bent
    To see how this footstool was made.

Joseph got caught in a college one year
    And I was detained in a jail
We fell in with evil companions I fear
    And learned evil ways — being frail.

But Joe — well, they left him a fortune, poor duck,
    Which blighted his life at the root
And I — well, it's always the Irish for luck —
    Fell heir to a wandering foot.

So Joey and I have large leisure to think —
    We two — not counting the sex —
Wherefore we admire to consider the gink —
    Or maybe he's bohunk[3] or Mex.

Maybe he's bohunk or Lettish[4] or Russ
    Maybe he's Yankee or Turk
Yet one big raw item divides him from us:
    His low disposition to work.

But Joe and I have our distinguishing marks,
    For he doesn't work 'cause he won't,
And me? — Well, I'm one of those sensitive sharks,
    So I never work 'cause I don't.

Why should we toil when the world keeps us prime
    With nothing but loafing to do
While yonder the fisherman toils over time
    And works good and plenty for two.

For two — and the ladies, God bless 'em and more,
    Who keep us from want and from lack
With Joe prancing proudly in through the front door
    And me chasing 'round to the back.

For Providence succors the lowly and spurned
    But Providence sometimes has pets,
And gives Joe and me what we never have earned
    While the gink, he earns more than he gets.

We are the social triangle of old
    Luxury, labor and vice;
Joe requires me and my strong arm to hold
    The gink at his work for the price.

Oh, the gink is the gink though works at his job
    In office, mine, shop, ship or field,
Whoever produces — him Joe and I rob,
    No matter how princely his yield.

The work of his hands or his brain or his soul —
    His trade, his profession, his art —
We take our tariff, we measure our dole
    From bank and from peddler's cart.

Sir Joe picks a million poor-pockets by law,
    I prey on the few who are rich.
His wants are complex and they gripe and they gnaw,
    My few frugal needs only itch.

We're welded and clinched by the world's surest tie
　　That binds thieves together in peace:
Joe strips all the ginks of their birthrights while I
　　Try out Joey's leavings[5] for grease.

So I loll me down by the sea while it sleeps
　　And pull my hat over my eyes
And thank my good stars for the order that keeps
　　Us three in our paradise:

The gink by the kelp and Sir Joseph and me,
　　Not counting the lady in red,
For we are the world as it really should be
　　All sheltered, accoutred[6] and fed.

Good Lord, let the worker out there in the boat
　　Pull in with it filled to the brim,
But give us who loaf all the fish he can float
　　With never a sardine for him.

With never a smelt[7] for a gink or the dutch,
　　The guinnea,[8] the mick[9] or the coon,[10]
The wap[11] or the whiteman[12] or Johnnie[13] or such
　　As moil[14] through the long afternoon.

So let us sprawl here by the slumbering tide
　　All lazy and idle and warm —
Joseph and me and the gay peroxide[15] —
　　But God help us all in the storm!

(Unpublished, typed copy, signed. William Allen White Collection, Emporia State University Library. Published with permission of Barbara White Walker. • 1. An absurd, eccentric person. • 2. Any of various large brown seaweeds. • 3. A derogatory term for a Hungarian immigrant, or for an inferior lout. • 4. The Letts belonged to a Balto-Slavic culture, closely related to Lithuanians. • 5. Human refuse, offal. • 6. To clothe or equip. • 7. Any of certain small food fishes. • 8. A derogatory term for an immigrant of Italian or Spanish origin. • 9. An Irishman or a Roman Catholic. • 10. American slang for a Negro. • 11. Italian immigrants. • 12. A man belonging to a race of European extraction. • 13. A nick-name humorously applied to assorted classes of men. • 14. To work hard. • 15. Hair bleached with hydrogen peroxide.)

COLLEGE DAYS

Friends and Brothers

The human soul pent up alone,
    As if entombed within the breast,
    Consumes itself in dull unrest,
And lost is life's sweet over-tone.
    Our better selves we should not hide
        Behind a mask from others,
    To strangers we should not confide
        But to our friends and brothers.

Unselfish noble thoughts engage
    Minds joined by strong fraternal ties;
    For Charity with tear-dimmed eyes
Heeds not the blot on Friendship's page.
    The lowly Nazarene hath said
        To men: "Love one another."
    The thorniest path we lightly tread
        When with a friend or brother.

The true fraternity is found,
    Not in the self-conceited clan,
    But where true manhood makes the man,
And kindness and good will abound.
    In our society we aim,
        That each shall help the others;
    Phi Delta Theta's highest claim
        Is that of friends and brothers.

Perhaps the future years will bring
    Cessation from this wrangling strife,
    Which we in ignorance call Life.
And deeds from generous impulse spring,
    Then shall our own fraternity,
        Surviving all the others,
    Initiate humanity
        And call men friends and brothers.

(University Review, University of Kansas, IX, February 1888, 140.)

To the Class of Eighty-Nine
(Tune — Upidee)

Once there was a Senior Class, K.S.U., K.S.U.
Who did their hard exams all pass, down at K.S.U.
They felt so glad when they got through,
They feasted Profs, and Juniors too.

Chorus:

    K.S., K.S., K.S.U. Gold and blue, high and true,
    K.S., K.S., K.S.U. Grand old K.S.U.
    Rock-chalk-jayhawk — K.U.
    K.S., K.S., K.S.U. Gold and blue, high and true,
    K.S., K.S., K.S.U. Eighteen-eighty nine.

This mighty class of '89, K.S.U., K.S.U.
Will soon go in the world to shine, shine for K.S.U.
E'en now they have their armor on
And soon from us they will be gone.
Chorus.

Their grades are good, their records clean
As any class these halls have seen, halls of K.S.U.
And may success in worldly strife,
Come to them as in college life.
Chorus.

Our hopes go with you '89, K.S.U., K.S.U.
For soon we'll follow in your line out of K.S.U.
Where e'er you be, what e'er you do
May you be an honor to —
Chorus.

(University Review, University of Kansas, XI, September 1889, 19.)

A July Jingle

Over the Valleys and over the plains,
    Over the hills comes the south wind sweet,
Filtered through woodlands and hedge-bordered lanes,
    Kissing the brooks and caressing the wheat.
South winds that blow from the billowy clover
    Flakes of faint perfume like ocean spray;
What is the tune that you keep humming over,
    What are the words you are trying to say?

"The air I am singing I took from the reaper,
    Murmuring drowsily far away,
Like a dream tune to the ear of the sleeper
    Comes my low song at the close of the day;
Timed by the tinkle of bells from the wood lot,
    Meadow larks singing the interlude slow,
Rests filled with voices so soft that you could not
    Doubt that they come from the spring house below."

(University Review {University of Kansas}, XI {September 1889}, 19.)

The Class Song of '90

She's my Alma Mater true:
I'm a graduate from K.S.U.
Soon we'll sever ne'er to part.
But in her halls and stately walls
You'll find —

Air: *"Little Annie Rooney:*

My heart is like the sunflower,
Our emblem thro' and thro';
It turns toward the progress
They make at K.S.U. —
Where all wear gold and blue,

Air: *"Annie Laurie"*

181

And all are bold and true.
My heart turns to'ard the progress
They made at —

K.S.U., a jolly place   Air: *"Mary's Little Lamb"*
She leads the race,
Without a trace
Of perspiration on her face,
But don't speak of base ball.

Chorus:
     Don't speak of base ball, at all, at all,
     At least not till next fall, down at K.S. —

You may listen for the ding dong,   Air: *"Ding Dong, Ding Dong,"*
Ding Dong of the bell,   *Chimes of Normandy*
In the recitation that you don't know well;
It's so long in coming, why you cannot tell;
But you wish the ding dong, ding dong we're in —

Held as my fondest recollection,   Air: *"Chorus of 'Lullaby for*
     Are the college days that we've past,   *Ermine' "*
Oh could some kindle fairy stay them
     Stay them ere they flow so fast.
          Heigh ho!
             We know
                Not how fast they go,

           And Oh!
        Time seemed so slow,
But now has come the hour for starting:
     Let them before we go
Take on a memory of our parting
     One old song of long ago.

Sing verse or two (to taste as the cook book says), of Son of a
Gambolier and continue with these words to same tune.

We are the class of ninety,
  We come from K.S.U.
We're powerful smart and mighty —
  In grades we're quite a few;
And if you want to see a class
    That never a fly or flew
      Could buzz about,
        Why turn and shout
      For "Ninety K.S.U."
Chorus.
We're a lot of original packages, done up for Kansas trade,
And when the State's absorbed us she'll be pretty full I'm afraid.
So all you Eastern colleges — shut up for the next decade,
And watch the class of ninety march out on dress parade.

        As gay and festive freshmen
          We donned our giddy hats,
        As sophomores we were most at home,
          In killing time and cats;
        But when we bloomed to Juniors,
          With pink and peacock blue,
        Old eighty-nine with plugs so fine
          Were driven from the U.

(*University Review,* University of Kansas, XI, June 1890, 290.)

————

The Gradgerratun' o' Joe

Way down crost the medder an' cow lot,
  Thro' paths made by cattle an' sheep,
Where, cooled in the shade by the tall ellums made,
  The old crick has curled up to sleep
Down there where the wind sighun' mingles
  I'th prattelun' waters at play,

An' the coo coo coo of the turtle dove too,
　　Seeps in from the dim far away;
Down there by the banks of the Willer —
　　In spring where the sweet-williams grow —
'Twas at this place 'at he, all the time used to be:
　　The home of our little boy Joe.
　　　　　My Oh —
　　　　　　　How long ago.

Nope; none a' you couldn't a' know'd him,
　　Way back there in seventy-four,
When Idy an' me concluded 'at we
　　U'd edjicate Joe, rich or pore.
I mind how we skrimped, scraped an' worried,
　　An' how our first Christmas was dim,
An' how mother cried when we had to decide,
　　We couldn't send nothun' to him.
An' nobody else dreams the sorrow,
　　'At Idy an' me'd undergo,
A livun' that way all alone ever' day
　　A yernun' an' longun' fer Joe.
　　　　　High Oh
　　　　　　　Long ago.

So Idy an' me went together
　　To hear little Joe gradgerrate;
Little Joe did I say? meant big, anyway;
　　He spoke on the subject of "Fate."
An' "my, but the effort was splendid."
　　The folks said 'at set by my side,
But I never hyurd a sentence er word —
　　An' mother jest broke down an' cried.
I hadn't the heart fer to ask her
　　What was the matter, you know;
Fer I felt she'd a' said: "Our baby is dead,
　　I want back my own little Joe:
　　　　　Our Joe
　　　　　　　Of long ago."

So foller me down thro' the cow lot —
    Thro' paths worn by cattle an' sheep,
To where in the shade, by the tall ellums made,
    The old crick is tucked in to sleep;
Where sighs of the tired breeze whisper
    To quiet the waters at play;
An' the dreamy coo coo of the turtle dove true,
    Frightens care phantoms away;
For I like to set hyur a thinkun'!
    An' astun' the waters 'at flow,
What's come o' the dear little boy 'at played here
    In the days o' the long ago?
       Our Joe;
        High ho!

(*El Dorado Republican,* November 21, 1890; University of Kansas, *University Review* XII {December 1890}, 99-100; *Rhymes by Two Friends,* 161-63; *Kansas City Star,* March 26, 1894; J.H. Powers, *Some Emporia Verse,* 1910; *Sunflowers: a Book of Kansas Poems,* 1916, 130-32.)

A Little College Song

A little smile,
Then after while
A meeting at the ball;
A waltz or so
And then they go —
Acquaintances — that's all.

A little talk
A quiet walk,
A shady little street;
A little grate,
A little late,
A fender full of feet.

A Sunday call;
A dusky hall,
A blur of everything;
Four eyes, four lips
In sweet eclipse,
Behind an angel's wing.

A day in June
Come all too soon;
A badly spoken piece;
A tender sigh,
A long goodbye,
A trunk and a valise.

A square envel-
Ope and a fel-
Ow busy as can be;
A little year,
A little tear,
A little memory.

(*Emporia Gazette,* June 8, 1895; *The Weekly Gazette,* June 13, 1895)

MUSIC

Orpheus on Willer Creek

We pore folks down in Willer Crick
    Haint time to throw away
In music sich as 'em 'at's rich
    Can learn to sing and play.
We're middlin' at fiddlin';
    Though mostly it's by rote;
But sing a hymn an' beat the time
    Down-left-right-up by note.
They's 'em 'at runs to 'cordeons,
    An' them 'at choose the drum,
But my fav'rite, a gash-ding sight
    Is our melodeum.[1]

Its wheezin' tone I'll have to own,
    Ain't good for operays;
Yet after all I like its drawlin'
    Good ol' fashion ways;
'Taint made to play them bang away
    An' highty-tighty tunes.
'At greet the ears and catch the cheers,
    In furrin French saloons —
But jest you start "Take back the heart"
    Er say, "Sweet Belle Mahome" —
They're hard to beat, and twice as sweet
    On our melodeum

An' so of nights before the lights
    Are lit, I like to bring
My chair 'an sit a little bit
    An' have my Idy sing
Some ol' love song I learnt her long
    Before her mother went;
Fer 'en it seems like golden dreams
    Drip from thet instrument,
An' wake agin a voice 'ats bin,
    Fer many a long year — dumb,
'At talks an' cheers my lonely years
    From HER melodeum.

(*El Dorado Republican,* May 9 , 1890; *The Lance,* May 31, 1890. • 1. Melodeon, a small reed organ that has suction bellows to draw air inwards through the reeds.)

Jes' Like Him

Onct a man named Jimmy Sellers
    Lived on Willer Crick;
An' fer all yer funny fellers,
    He jes' took the trick.
Kep' a rester'nt where the Hewins
    Boardin' house now is;
An' at ev'ry show er doin's,
    Seller's geenyus ris:
Blacked up onct and played the nigger;
    'Nother time the star, —
Some they lowed he was a bigger
    Man 'en Booth by far.
So we never was exactun' —
    Let Jim have his way;
At his cuttun' up an' actun'
    Folks 'u'd only say:
"Jes' like him,
    That dag on Jim."

Used to set an' play the gitar
    Shady afternoons,
Till the strings 'u'd fairly glitter
    With his witchy tunes.
I kin almost see him playun'
    Ol' Seebantypool:
Both eyes shut an' him a swayun'
    Like a gash ding fool,
Y'orte hyurd him sing "Lorena"
    Er "Sweet Belle Mahome";
I tell you I never seen a
    Feller 'at could come
Nearder to a angel singun'
    'En Jim Sellers could;
Ef yer eyes 'u'd not be ringun'

Wet, yer feeluns' would —
Jes' like Jim —
Dag on him.

One time when a show was playun'
    In the court-house hall,
Jim he set there without sayun'
    Anything at all.
When 'twas done one of them wimmun
    Met Jim on the street;
An' we hyrun him plead with brimmun'
    Eyes; hyrun him entreat
Her to come back; hyrun him tell her
    How they'd both forget;
An' I never seen a feller
    Seem so grieved, an' yet,
When we'd ever cod or joke him
    Jim 'u'd laff and say,
In a voice 'at 'most 'u'd choke him:
    "I was drunk that day."
        Jes' like him —
        That dag on Jim.

(*El Dorado Republican,* December 25, 1891; *Kansas City Journal,* December 13, 1891; *Rhymes by Two Friends,* 172-74.)

Terpsicore on Willer Creek

The daughters of Terpsicore[1] who sit at Pallas'[2] feet,
    And overlook the festival of dancing,
In point of style and makeup may be very hard to beat —
As supple, soft-eyed houris[3] they're entrancing,
        But a tanned cheeked deity,
        Living in the Used-to-be,
Could beat these maids with cards and spades in bloom;
            For she reigned on Willer Crick
            and presided fair and chic,
O'er the "rags"[4] we used to give before the boom.[5]

The "rags' we used to give before we platted out the place,
    Before we had the opry house to splurge in,
Were free and easy gatherings of home-made country grace,
    And everybody came without the urgin';
        Oh, the fiddle and the horn,
        And the organ, wheezed and worn,
Made an itchy, twitchy, music in the gloom
        Of the busy work-a-day
        So that sorrow stayed away
From the "rags" we used to give before the boom.

The caller-off and fiddler was a simple homely soul
    Who had one waltz in all his repertory;
His long suit was his "cowdrills"[6] and the ever-flowing bowl[7]
    And the "Irish Washerwoman" was his glory.
        But he tickled up our heels
        With his old Virginia reels
Like an airy joyful fairy in the room;
        For then none of us were rich,
        Nor were parvynew[8] and sich —
At the "rags" we used to give before the boom.

(Kansas City Star, October 8, 1892; *Rhymes by Two Friends* {1893}, 223-24. • 1. The

muse of dancing and choral song. • 2. See the poem, "A Tribute to Jackson" for description of the Priests of Pallas festivals in Kansas City. • 3. A beautiful, white-skinned, black-eyed woman. • 4. "Rags" were acting events of boisterous merrymaking, such as stage and burlesque shows of a later date. • 5. The fast economic growth of the late 1880s. • 6. Quadrilles: music for a popular, 19th-century square dance of five figures, usually in 6/8 or 2/4 time. • 7. Likely an allusion to an alcoholic punch bowl. • 8. Parvenu: upstart people risen from a lower social station.)

After While

There was a day when anguish gashed my heart,
    And fevered grief throbbed through my frenzied brain,
    And beat upon my soul a rhythmed strain,
That echoed in the songs that used to start
Whene'er I touched the lute-strings of my art.
    O sad sweet songs that sorrow keyed to pain,
    And timed to dripping heart-blood and the rain
Of unwashed tears, that you and I should part.

That day is gone; I cannot strike the chords
    That sobbed of woe they vainly would conceal;
    Nor does my numbed heart quiver 'neath its thongs.
To-day dry eyes scan only empty words,
    A soul balmed in content can scarcely feel;
      Since comfort stemmed my wounds and stilled the songs.

(Rhymes by Two Friends, 214.)

A Song for Mistress Sylvia

Who is Sylvia? What is she,
That all our swains commend her?
— *Two Gentlemen of Verona*

I fain would sing to Sylvia a halting rhyme or two,
    With a high ho lawsy daisy, high ho hum,
For other bards have sung her praises since the lyre was new,
    Singing hey and lack-a-day until the bright days come.
And when he sings to Sylvia, each singer whispers low,
    A name he dare not weave into his melody, and so,
Fair Sylvia has charms from all the goddesses ago,
    Sing a hay and lack-a-daisy with a high ho hum.

O every song to Sylvia by lover ever writ,
    With a high ho lawsy daisy, high ho hum,
Is sweeter far than silence though it jars a little bit,
    Singing hey and lack-a-day until the bright days come.
For having loved and told of it, and having tried to sing,
    What matters if the trembling note hath not a golden ring;
O joy hath breathed on some lorn heart to move that dusty string,
    With its hey and lack-a-daisy and its high ho hum.

So I fain would sing to Sylvia a halting rhyme or two,
    With a high ho dearie, dearie high ho hum,
A-sighing words to Sylvia my heart would say to you,
    Singing hey and lack-a-day until the bright days come.
This song is made for you, my love, whose name is whispered low,
    This heart and voice are trembling as this husky tune doth flow;
And her who knows she's Sylvia — this world may never know,
    Singing hey ho dearie, dearie high ho hum.

(Rhymes by Two Friends, 217-18; Kansas City Star, June 26, 1893.)

The Music Which "Hath Charms"

"Such songs have power to quiet,
The restless pulse of care."

Before we moved from Willer Crick our Idy used to play,
Her organ in the sittun room thro' all the live-long day.
The pieces that she liked the most was "Trippun Thro' the Dells,"
An' "Siegel's March," an' "Shepherd Boy," an' "Monastery Bells."
She knowed the "Cornflow'r Waltz" without a-lookun at a note.
An' sang "When You and I Were Young" out of her head by rote.
Her pieces long ago had tears, an' tunes a man could hum,
But her piany music now goes frizzle, whimble, bum!
T'was writ by furrin labor either "ustski," "off" or "iski,"
An' a man — I think she calls him Glasowhiski.

She used to play the second — made it up y' understand —
While I sawed on the fiddle "Ol' Zip Coon" or "Buly land."
We used to have a medley-piece that gave her ma a pain,
Of "Devil's Hornpipe," "Martin's Hymn" and "Whoop Up Lizy Jane";
An' me an' Ide 'u'd play it jest to hyur ma grunt round,
'N'en change to "Annie Laurie," till we'd hyur a snuffin sound;
An n'en we knowed 'at ma fergot, an' banished every care —
But law! them days is over — you jest mighty right they air;
Now when her daddy asts about some piece she plays so frisky —
It's "Why, pa, that's a thing from Glasowhiski."

That Glasowhiski feller — or whatever is his name —
Has broke into the temple where they keep the thing called fame;
Him an' the man called Motzart, an' Baytoven, an' Goono,[1]
An' maybe half a dozen more that Idy raves on so.
But I'm still fer "Lorena" or "They'll Be One Vacant Chair" —
The songs that cuddle up an' kiss dry lips of mem'ries fair,
An' make 'em smile again; but then — each feller to his taste,
So if them haint dimons then I hanker after paste.
But Idy she's fergot 'em — ef I call for one it's risky —
    It's "Listen to this thing from Glasowhiski."

(Rhymes by Two Friends, 178-80; also published as "The Old Songs" in *Pointers* (Kansas City Missouri), XVII {April 1911}, 50. • 1. Charles Gounod {1818-1893}, composed opera, *Faust,* in 1859.)

A Side Talk with Calliope

Come hither, come hither, O timorous muse,
　　Come hither, O trembling lass:
Your Pegasus[1] hobbles without any shoes,
　　Come out of the tall tangled grass.
A green fungus hides the Pierian[2] spring
　　Where frog choirs nightly rehearse,
And, perched on the sunken lyre's cynical string,
　　They croak their society verse.
Come out of the brush, O sweet heavenly maid,
　　Come out, dainty beauty, and say
What bellowing mortal hath made you afraid,
　　What clumsy clown chased you away.

"And it's how can I, how can I, how can I sing,
　　How can I sing to your race;
A race that has scorned every chivalric thing
　　And put patent gears in its place?
O Mercury[3] now has a pneumatic tire,
　　And Psyche[4] has donned crinoline;
A new smoke consumer adorns Vulcan's[5] fire,
　　And Clio[6] writes on a machine;
Poor Cupid[7] mayn't shoot with his arrow and bow
　　On the town-site I fear before long.
Then why should I serve at the beck of my foe,
　　Why should I hallow this wrong?"

O the half gods are gone, so hurrah for the gods,
　　The gods of the order that is,
And here's to the cycle of commerce and clods,
　　And here's to the health of "old biz."
Then we'll larrup[8] the lyre with the trace-chains[9] of trade
　　And dance to the jangling din;
We'll gladly excuse you, sweet Heavenly maid,
　　But run your old Pegasus in;

We'll sell your old nag for what his bones will bring
    To click in the minstrelsee,[10]
And rattle them off to the ditty we sing
    That tells us how clever are we.

(Kansas City Star, March 7, 1894. • 1. From Greek mythology, a winged horse which leaped from Medusa when she died. • 2. A fountain in Pieria, a place in ancient Macedonia and supposedly sacred to the Muses, and believed to inspire writing of poetry. • 3. A carrier, messenger or guide who ran on foot — but now rides on rubber car or bicycle tires. • 4. A beautiful princess in classical mythology with whom Cupid, Venus' son, fell in love. • 5. The Roman god of fire. • 6. The muse of history in Greek mythology. • 7. The Roman god of love. • 8. To beat upon with strong blows. • 9. Two chains of a harness to attach a horse to a vehicle. • 10. Bones were manually clicked together to produce rhythm in a minstrel show. Calliope, in Greek mythology, was the Muse who presided over eloquence and heroic poetry.)

Four Songs of Songs

Just One Song

Just let me sing one song;
    Dear Lord, just one
Sweet heart-throb clear and strong,
    In unison
With strains I've lisped so long,
    And I am done.

Just let me touch one chord
    Before I go;
Just let me leave some word,
    That men may know
How sweet life is; dear Lord,
    I love it so.

I ask not that this name
    Continue long,
An empty shell preserved by fame;
    Dear Lord, among
These husks, doomed for the flame
    Save just one song.

(Kansas City Star, May 27, 1894. The first of four poems in "Four Songs of Songs.")

Apollo on Willer Crick

Well, well now jest you listen to that dad-blamed organ play
A song that I hain't heard for — O, it's many a long day.
"Sweet Evelina" — well, well, well, if that don't beat the Jews![1]
I'd plumb fergot it slick and clean and yet I used to lose
My head and heart — a singin' it there! hear it? hear it sigh?
"My love for you," how does it go? "will never, never die."
There's a real true "Evelina" somewhere, if she's living yet,
I sang to in high tenor in the Arion Quartette.[2]

That Arion Quartette — why I ain't thought a thing of it
For years and years; I wonder if I'm just a little bit
Well — harder, say — than some would be; I bet Ed Harvey thinks
And Herm and Lew about them times, and Charley — yess — 'y jinks
I wonder if the girls we used to serenade reflect
At hearin' "Evelina" in a — well — a retrospect.
I wonder if they hear my voice, and smile — or just forget
The way I sang the tenor in the Arion Quartette.

Them nights — my! my! them moonlight nights — seem like they
    always was
A floatin' 'round in tenderness like quince[3] preserves in sauce!
And how we swigged that tenderness 'till each ached to go
And serenade his own girl first, but dassent[4] let on though.
"Sweet Evelina," who'd a thought that you would ever be
In what our Idy's essay calls the Caves of Memory.[5]
"Sweet Evelina" — well — our love did die — for all — and yet
I'm glad I sang the tenor in the Arion Quartette.

(*Kansas City Star,* May 27, 1894, 7; the second of White's poems in "Four Songs of Songs." • 1. Colloquial for "doesn't that beat all!" • 2. The Arion Quartette was the forerunner of the University of Kansas Glee Club. During White's years at KU, Arion's members were: Charles F. Scott, later editor of the *Iola* (Kansas) *Register,* and his brother, Angelo, Willis Gleed and Scott Hopkins. • 3. Quince, an apple-like fruit used for marmalade, jelly and preserves. • 4. *i.e.,* does not. • 5. Long-forgotten memories of what had been experienced or learned were once thought to be stored in hollow chambers of the mind.)

The Song of a Song

A certain singer in the early days
Made him a ballad for his sweetheart's praise,
He put in it such lines of loving truth,
That his brow burned at scanning them; forsooth
He dared not place it 'neath her maiden eyes,
In his bold scrawl, for fear she might despise
His halting rhymes; wherefore a practiced clerk
Illumed his lay,[1] with many a curl and quirk.

> *When we are gone, what of this love of ours,*
> > *Sweetheart, dear heart and true?*
> *Is it like beauty, dying with the flowers?*
> *Will it die too?*

So toiled and moiled[2] the aged clerk and grim;
For work was work; it was no song to him.
The lover took the scroll whereon was writ
His ditty, and with shy pride carried it,
And put it snugly in the trysting[3] tree,
Where honeyed notes were sometimes changed; and she,
That sweetheart, marveled only at the work,
Which had been wrought so finely by the clerk.

> *Is love not real, as real and quick as life,*
> > *Sweetheart, trueheart, and dear?*
> *And loveless who would fear death's cruel knife;*
> > *And linger here?*

The maiden laid the parchment by in myrrh,
It was a keepsake, not a song to her.
And time trudged on along its weary way;
The singer died; forgotten was his lay.
Well, so it happed in conning old tomes[4] o'er,
Within a dingy shop where mouldered refuse lore,
A woman with a widowed heart came on
These rhymes of that old day so long agone.

> *O, love will live thro' death, thro' death, thro' death.*
> > *Sweetheart, — dear heart, and true;*

And should God first call back this weary breath,
    I'll wait for you.

Then with that woman hope dwelled sweet and strong,
The olden rhymes at last became a song.

(Kansas City Star, May 27, 1894, 7. Third poem of four in "Four Songs of Songs" by White. • 1. Hand-illuminated his work. • 2. Hard work, drudgery. • 3. An appointed meeting place. • 4. A book.)

The Chords in C

Just the simple chords in C,
    Idly thrummed here in the shade
    To some song or serenade,
Or some broken melody,
    Drifting from I know not where
    Caught and held as in a snare
By the simple chords in C —
All I know of harmony.

Just the simple chords in C,
    Twanged here in this tilted chair
    On the blue-grass, while the air
    Pulses with the throbbing whir
Of the locust in the tree;
    And field noises jangled, blur
With the tunes that come to me.
Thrumming simple chords in C.

Oh; the simple chords in C
    Fit the pieces that I know;
    They are simple pieces, though —
Love song, ballad, dirge, and glee;
    Made for simple folks to sing,
    Filled with cadences that bring
Tender thrills of memory,
When I pick the chords in C.

Just the simple chords in C,
    In what unison they seem
With the humming of the bee
    And the laughter of the stream;
    While the voices of the day,
    Mingled notes of work and play,
Rhyme in one sweet rhapsody,
With the simple chords in C.

Just the simple chords in C,
    Through what countless years have they
    Murmured as they sigh today
Out here in the grass to me.
    Oh, what hearts now dust have met
    'neath some moonlit minaret,
Met and danced in ecstacy,
To the simple chords in C,

Just the simple chords in C,
    Have been strong enough to move
    Hearts to joy and hope and love,
    They have done and they will do,
For the ages yet to be;
    They are lowly, it is true,
Are those simple chords in C,
Yet they're good enough for me.

So I drum the chords in C,
    Out here in the shadows flit
    With the wayward winds and knit
Angel dreams in filigree,
    Here I sit ashamed to try
    Tunes that go a-spinning by,
So I fancy songs that be,
Timed to simple chords in C.

(Agora, 3 no. 4 (April 1894), 276-77. *Kansas City Star,* May 27, 1894, 7. The fourth poem in "Four Songs of Songs.")

To the Raven

What though they tell me all my melodies were sung,
By olden singers in some long forgotten tongue,
Go tell the lover loving is as old as time,
'Twill still his impulses as thy words will still my rhyme.

(Kansas City Star, December 16, 1894)

———

Before the Daybreak

Before the daybreak shines a star
    That in the day's great glory fades;
Too fiercely bright is the full light
    That her pale-gleaming lamp upbraids.
Before the daybreak sings a bird
    That stills her song ere morning light;
Too loud for her is the day's stir,
    The woodland's thousand-tongued delight,
Ah! great the honor is, to shine
    A light wherein no traveler errs,
And rich the prize, to rank divine
    Among the world's best choristers.
But I would be that paler star,
    And I would be that lonlier bird;
To shine with hope, while hope's afar,
    And sing of love when love's unheard.

(Kansas City Star, April 19, 1895.)

CHILDREN

King's Ex[1]

"When the wood is brought in an' the chores 're all done, at the dusk,
   an' the dyin' day
Kisses the world a smilin' farewell, ere the night has come in to pray.
The children romp out in the sunflower weeds, in Simmons's vacant
   lot,
Maybe they're playin' at hide-and-go-seek, er pull-away jes' like es not;
Fer the games 'at they have never change very much, ner they never
   git more complex —
An' I'm glad in my heart 'at the children hold on to the old-fashioned
   sayin': 'King's Ex.'

"Little boy, as you go crost the breakin' of life, when your voice shall
   grow rougher an' deep;
When the cares of the day make you stumble an' trip, an' pile on you
   when you're asleep;
When you walk in the path when you ortent to step, an' feel yourse'f
   goun to fall;
When no one's around fer to hold to a bit, where yer own little
   strength is so small;
Like a child all alone cryin' out in the night, when you've got on yer
   dark blue specs,[2]
You'll clasp yer hands then, as you cross fingers now, and pray fer a
   sweet King's Ex.

"Little girl, though they call you a tom-boy to-day, to-morrow they'll let
   out your dress;
An' with every flounce an' each ruffle an' braid, a joy an' a care comes,
   I guess.
Some day in the big unknown future, perhaps, you'll taste the vile
   dregs in the glass
You drank from so wildly an' blindly an' mad, your hand could not
   yield it to pass.
When you feel, in your bitterness, sorrow an' shame, the cruel stones
   thrown at your sex;
When men shall be deaf to your piteous cry — ask God for a little
   King's Ex."

(*Kansas City Journal,* April 25, 1892, in an editorial column entitled, "A Salina Instance." *Rhymes by Two Friends,* 186-87, J.H. Powers, ed., *Some Emporia Verse,* 1910. • 1. "King's Ex" was a cry to stop a game or a fight; to prevent one's self from being caught in a game of tag. • 2. Blue-glass spectacles, used here with the same meaning as today's expression, "Rose-colored glasses.")

Father's Little Joke

Father used to rig the girls about us bein' pore,
An' go on lots about things what's a go'n to happen shore;
The hot winds an' the hoppers an' the chinchbugs in the wheat,
An' holler-horn an' ten-cent corn; — you never seen the beat
Of how he used to grunt around — jest gasin like, you see —
"We're goin' to the pore-house, Sue, lickety-split," sezee.
Then, snappin' of his galluses[1] an' backin' to the fire,
He'd stretch an' smile a little while and puff his reekin' briar;
An' takin' in the sittun room from every which-a-way,
"This is good enough fer pore folks," is what father'd always say.

F'r instunce say some Sunday when the Ruggleses drove down; —
Unload a hull darn wagon full; jes' like a small-sized town;
An' father'd look at mother an' he'd ast her if she's got
That johnny-cake and side of bacon left — es like es not.
Then mother'd tie her apron on an' guess that she'd make out: —
(T'u'd do you good if you jest could see mother fly about.)
Well — they'd be mashed potatoes, chicken, turnips, squash an' slaw,
Tomato stew an' string-beans too, perserves an' pie an' — law,
Dead codles[2] of brown gravy; an' nen — after father'd pray —
"This is good enough fer pore folks," is what father'd always say.

The night Jane come home cryin', when they give her her divorce,
The girls an' me an' mother we made over her a-course;
But father stayed around the barn an' mother passed the plates,
When supper come an' made up somethin' 'bout his fixin' gates.
Then after supper father came an' set around an' smoked,
An' looked at Jane time an' again, 'zif he'd a-like to joked
An' churped her up, but dassent 'n' yet wanted her to know

How glad he was she'd come to us, but couldn't jest say so.
At bedtime father pinched Jane's cheeks — his dear old-fashioned way—
"Home's good enough fer pore folks," was all father's voice could say.

(*Rhymes by Two Friends,* 206-208; *Kansas City Star,* April 4, 1894. • 1. Suspenders or braces. • 2. Dead coddles: a noun colloquially derived from the transitive verb, "to coddle," or hot bowls of gravy.)

————

A Wail in B Minor

Oh, what has become of the ornery boy,
    Who used to chew slip'ry elm, "rosum" and wheat:
And say "jest a coddin' " and "what d'ye soy";
    And wear rolled-up trousers all out at the seat?

And where is the boy who had shows in the barn,
    And "skinned a cat backwards" and turned "summersets";
The boy who had faith in the snake-feeder yarn,
    And always smoked grapevine and corn cigarettes?

Where now is the small boy who spat on his bait,
    And proudly stood down near the foot of the class,
And always went "barefooted" early and late,
    And washed his feet nights on the dew of the grass?

Where is the boy who could swim on his back,
    And dive and tread water and lay his hair, too;
The boy who would jump off the spring-board kerwhack,
    And light on his stomach as I used to do?

Oh where and oh where is the old-fashioned boy?
    Has the old-fashioned boy with his old-fashioned ways
Been crowded aside by the Lord Fauntleroy, —
    The cheap tinseled make-believe, full of alloy
    Without the pure gold of the rollicking joy
Of the old-fashioned boy in the old-fashioned days?

(*Rhymes by Two Friends,* 188-89; *Kansas City Star,* March 2, 1894; William Allen White, *The Court of Boyville,* New York: McClure, Phillips, 1902 {2}.)

A GROUP OF HUMBLE CRADLE SONGS

A Willer Crick Lullabye

O Lissun an' hush-a-bye, while daddy sings,
    Bylo, pa's littul man, do;
An' ma reds the table an' clears up the things,
    Bylo, pa's littul man, do.
I'll make up a song fer you out of my head,
About all the fairies what's livun er dead;
An' if you go bylo, I'll bet 'tull come true,
    Bylo, pa's littul man, do.

Two littul boys onct went to bed in a loft,
    Bylo, pa's little man, do;
An' both of 'em heerd purty music as soft,
    As Bylo, pa's littul man, do;
So one littul shaver jest shut his eyes tight,
An' played with the fairies the hull live-long night, —
The other'n who wouldn't heerd boogers go "boo!"
    Bylo, pa's littul man, do.

So run, littul tyke, with the fairies an' play,
    Bylo, pa's littul man, do —
Wood-tag, er bean-bag, er ol' pull away, —
    Bylo, pa's littul man, do.
They'll take you way up to a world above this,
An' let you slide down on the thread of a kiss,
With ma at the bottom a wakun' up you —
    Bylo, pa's littul man, do.

(*Kansas City Star,* July 15, 1893; *Rhymes by Two Friends,* 190-91, the first of three poems in "A Group of Humble Cradle Songs"; J.H. Powers, *Some Emporia Verse,* 1910.)

A Jim Street Lullabye

Hursh-a-bye, sweetheart,
   O, hursh an' lay still,
Mommer 'ull stay with you,
   Dear, come w'ot will;
Mommer c'u'd not live without you — my pet —
Mommer is proud of you — an' don' regret;
Gawd! how can some people want to ferget;
   Hursh-a-bye; sweet and lay still — dear.

Hursh-a-bye, sweet-heart,
   O hursh an' lay still;
Lookie at them purties
   There on the sill;
Dearie, them's posies, an' some day we'll go
Back to the ol' place where wild posies grow —
Jest us alone — shur they'll nobody know —
   Hursh-a-bye, sweet, an' lay still — dear.

Hursh-a-bye, sweet-heart,
   O hursh an' lay still;
Purtiest dreams
   May your littul heart fill.
W'y shouldn't they, like es not? and come true?
You hain't done nothin' rich babies don' do;
Me an' the angels an' Jesus loves you!
   Hursh-a-bye, sweet an' lay still — dear.

(Rhymes by Two Friends, 191-92, second of three poems in "A Group of Humble Cradle Songs." *Overland Monthly* (New York), 25, January 1895, 106.)

Sister Mary's Lullabye

Zhere, zhere, 'ittul b'o', sistuh'll wock you to s'eep,
    Hush-a-bye O, darlene, wock-a-bye b'o',
An' tell you the stowy about the b'ack sheep —
    Wock-a-bye my 'ittul b'over.
A boy onct said "b'ack sheep, you d'ot any wool?"
"Uh-huhm" said the lambie, "I dot free bags full."
An' where Murry went w'y the lamb's sure to doe,
They's mowe of zis stowy — I dess I don' know;
    But hush-a-bye O, darlene, wock-a-bye b'o',
      Wock-a-bye my 'ittul b'over.

O, mama says buddy tomed stwaight down f'om Dod;
    Hush-a-bye O, uh-huhm, wock-a-bye b'o',
'At doctuh mans bwunged him, now isn't shat odd —
    Wock-a-bye my 'ittul b'over.
For papa says, "Doctuhs is thiefs so zhey be."
An' thiefs tain't det up into Heaven you see!
I dess w'en one do's up an' dets sent below,
He's dot to bwing wif him a baby or so;
    Hush-a-bye O, uh-huhm, wock-a-bye b'o'.
      Wock-a-bye, my 'ittul b'over.

But sistuh loves b'o' anyhow if he's dood,
    Hush-a-bye O, sweetie, wock-a-bye b'o'.
Better'n tandy er infalid's food —
    Wock-a-bye sistuh's own b'over.
An' some day when buddy drows up to a man,
W'y sistuh an' him 'ull 'ist harness ol' Fan,
An' dwive off to Heaven the fuist zhing you know,
An' bwing over' baby back what wants to doe.
    Zhen hush-a-bye O, sweetie, wock-a-bye b'o',
      Wock-a-bye sistuh's own b'over.

(*Rhymes by Two Friends,* 192-94; The third of three poems in "A Group of Humble Cradle Songs." Also published as "Little Sister's Lullaby" in White's *The Court of Boyville* (1902), 180.)

"Bud" and the Hatchet Myth

Onct was a boy an' he couldn't lie;
No sir, no matter how he try.
N'en his dad w'y he up an' said:
"George git the wood 'fore you go to bed."
George didn't like it a bit 'adburn,
T' bring in the wood when it wasn't his turn;
But alles sames he mosied out,
Picked up his ax, an' he looked about
Wher was a churry tree 'at his dad
Bragged on what fine cherries it had.
N'en w'y George lit in an' chopped
The ol' tree down an' never stopped
Till he cut it into sticks so small,
Piled way up ginst the kitchen wall.
Well, purty soon his dad comed in,
Looked at his wood, an' said with a grin:
"George, who got all this nice wood?"
George didn't lie 'cause he never could —
But telled his dad jest the hones' fac's:
"I done it, sir, with my littul ax."

(Rhymes by Two Friends, 204-205; Kansas City Star, February 22, 1894.)

The New Wrinkle on Mr. Bill

I like it when they's company
Comes to visit us fer we
Gets to have the goodest things —
Ist like Sunday; 'n'en 'y jings,
Me and Wullie gets a chance
To wear our littul boughten pants —
Uncle Hiram give us when
He was here onct — ist like men.

Pa says, Wullie he's so dumb
'Bout behavin', he can't come
To the table any more:
'Cause Ma most went th'ue the floor,
T'other day, when Mrs. Gus
Vandergrif she et with us.
When we all got done with soup,
Wullie he sets up a hoop:
"Ma! come take my bowl away!
What 'you wunged that bell fer? Ay?"

(Rhymes by Two Friends, 202; *Kansas City Star,* March 27, 1894)

Womanhood

I kissed her baby, and its hazel eyes
Beamed through my soul, where in a dim recess,
There is a pictured face on which distress
Plays hide and seek with hope; a tear-drop dries,
Warmed by her parting smile; again she tries
To reach me with a pantomime caress.
This, I in my anguish had called "Raithlessness"[1]
And pricked it on my heart with poisoned dies.[2]

The baby's lips were sweet with drowsy wine
Pressed out of dreams, by fragrant fancies stirred.
I drank my fill and yielded to its mood.
And when I woke the picture still was mine;
(By baby lips the title has been blurred)
And underneath was written, "Womanhood."

(Rhymes by Two Friends, 212; *Kansas City Star,* March 12, 1895. • 1. i.e.,
"wrathlessness," or the antithesis of violent anger. • 2. The heart is here a poisoned
matrix either punched or shaped by deadly dies.)

A Little Dream — Boy

Little Boy Blue come blow your horn,
And wake up a little man lying forlorn,
Asleep where his life wanders out of the morn.

Little Boy Blue blow a merry, sweet note,
Over the pool where the white lilies float —
Fill out the sails of a little toy boat.

Blow on my dream of a little boy there —
Blow thro' his little bark-whistle, and snare
Your breath in a tangle of curly brown hair.

Blow and O blow from your fairy land far,
Blow while my little boy wears a tin star,
And rides a stick horse to a little boy's war.

Blow for the brave man my dream-boy would be,
Blow back his tears when he wakes up to see
His knight errant gone and instead — only me.

Little Boy Blue come blow your horn,
Blow for a little boy lying forlorn,
Asleep where his life wanders out of the morn.

(Rhymes by Two Friends, 156-57; *Kansas City Star,* November 10, 1893)

———

Mr. Bill's Insomnia

Littul Wullie — he's my brother —
 He hain't got a lick a sense.
Pa says Wullie's like his mother —
 He is ist so very dense.
Th' other morning Wullie's piller -

213

Case it had some holes in it;
An' we thought 'at ma 'u'd kill 'er
    Self a laffin fore she quit.
Pa, he says, "Geemy-my, Jenny,
    Tell us what you're laffin 'bout."
Ma says, "Wullie can't sleep any
    'Cause he says his dreams leak out."

(Rhymes by Two Friends, 203.)

The Silent Word

Out in the hard dirt path,
    That run 'round the house by the rain bar'l
And keeps the yard grass back
    From choking the morning glories,
Sits little brown-eyed Jane
    Singing her song to her playthings.

The wind has tumbled her hair,
    Running his fingers thro' it;
Cooling them may be as we
    Stretch our hands out to the south wind.
For Jane's fluffy tresses are dark;
    The wind perhaps thinks they are shadows.

Little Jane breathes the fresh air,
    And rocks in her little oak rocker,
Pouring her wild song out
    Tuned to her to-and-fro singing;
Timed to no tune save her joy —
    Joy that is keener than feeling.

One cannot follow her words;
    The words of her song nor their meaning,
The songs of the birds are sweet,
    The secrets the wind tells the poplars —
Secrets it gets from the grass
    The trees never whisper to mortals.

What are the verses the brook
        Rhythmically croons to the pebbles —
Lifeless stone dolls without ears
        Nor cheeks for the brook's fond caresses —
Pan[1] would not try to revamp
        These songs that mortals might sing them.

Yet with her lisping words —
        Words of familiar accents —
Little Jane sings the same songs
        The bird and the tree and the brook sing;
No one may capture these songs
        No one may sing or translate them.

Still there's a word in each heart
        One word that no lips have uttered,
One word that struggles for voice,
        This word holds all the songs' meaning;
Every heart pulses this word
        When joy throbs it sweet in iambics.[2]

Thus doth the song of a bird,
        The prattle of wind, wave or childhood,
Wake something quick in the soul,
        Something all hearts fain[3] would utter,
Something that strives for a voice,
        Something dumb mortals call longing.
                    * * * * *
Out in the hard dirt path,
        That runs 'round the house by the rain bar'l,
And keeps the yard grass back
        From choking the morning glories,
Sits little brown-eyed Jane,
        Singing a song to her playthings.

(*Kansas City Star,* August 30, 1893. A typescript copy is extant in the William Allen White collection in the Emporia State University Library, with its holographic title, "Little Browneyed Jane," but lacks the final stanza, which repeats the first. • 1. Pan was a Greek god of flocks and pastures and their wild life. • 2. Greek literary designation of a type of poetry, characterized by verses composed of iambic feet. • 3. Well-pleased or glad.)

A Lullaby for Lullabyers

O hush, callow lullaby singers and rest —
    Fol de rol, tra la la loo;
For babydom looks on your tribe as a pest —
    Fol de rol, tra la la loo.
We don't want our mamas to kiss us to sleep;
We don't care a pin if the shadows are deep;
We don't care a whoop for the lone watch you keep —
    Fol de rol, tra la la loo.

    Fol de rol, hiddlety tiddlety ted.
    Lullaby man's got a wheel in his head.
    Higglety pigglety — that's what he said!
    Fol de rol, tra la la loo.

We babies are sick of the gibbering gush —
    Fol de rol, tra la la loo —
The "mooning" and "Crooning" and "little one, hush" —
    Fol de rol, tra la la loo.
These bachelor cooers must let us alone;
Falsetto won't fool us nor will it alone
For not having younkers about of their own;
    Fol de rol, tra la la loo.

    Fol de rol, squillery squallery squirts
    Posing as mamas to pay for dress shirts —
    Hellity pellity, that is what hurts!
    Fol de rol, tra la la loo.

(Kansas City Star, September 2, 1893.)

———

The Strange Case of Mr. Edward
Mr. Charey Solus

I'm 'ist on'y got free cousins —
    'Ceptin' them 'at lives back East,
Pa he says they must be dozens

'Round Sandusky there at least —
On'y free, 'ist Sam an' Jennie —
    She's growed up an's got a beau —
'N', Eddie, he's my age, but 'en he
    Cries lots more 'en I do though.
When he's bad, Aunt May looks steady
    All around, 'ist ever'where,
'N' says: "Papa, where — is — Eddie?"
    Snarly — he's — got — Eddie's — chair!"

"Dear — me — suz," says Uncle Ellis,
    "Where — is — Eddie — any — way?"
"Snarly knows, but — he — won't — tell — us;
    No — sir — ee — bob!" says Aunt May.
"Nen we laugh an' Eddie doesn't
    Want to hush a tall an' quit.
First you know if Eddie wasn't
    Smilin' 'ist a teenty bit.
'Nen Aunt May asts: "Where — is — Snarly?
    Mercy — sakes — did — ever — you
See — the — like —? Now — Cousin — Charley!
    Hush er Eddie he'll laugh, too."

(Kansas City Star, October 27, 1893.)

The Nursery Handicap

Mary's riding Mr. Tiger; I'm a-riding pa;
We'll just have the biggest race you purt' near ever saw.
Only Tiger he's so bad, when Mary says "git dap!"
He lays down and sticks his nose in Aunt Eliza's lap.

When pa kites[1] out like a race horse what has broke its check,
All that little boys can do is grab him round the neck.
Pa he plays he's runned away when Mary wants to swap;
"Gee haw, pa, and wait for Mary; can't you never stop?"

217

This here horse will carry double cause he just said so;
Climb on, Mary! Hike there, hike there! That's the way to go!
Tige, hyuh, Tige, let Mary ride you, that's a good dog, do;
There's a nice old Tiger doggie, come and play, won't you?

Stop your laughing, Uncle Ellis; can't you never quit?
Pa just bumped his head a little — he ain't hurt a bit!
Mary's riding Mr. Tiger, I'm a-riding pa.
We'll just have the biggest race you purt' near ever saw.

(Kansas City Star, "Extra Sheet," February 17, 1894, 11. • 1. To fly or glide.)

———————

Elder Twigg's Cradle Song

High, baby, ho baby, shut your eyes tight,
Pappy will sing you a love song tonight —
Sing you a love song he sang long ago —
Sang to his sweetheart your pappy loved so;
Her eyes were like yourn that are peakin' so bright;
High baby, ho baby, shut your eyes tight.

High, baby, ho baby, that's a good girl,
Cuddle up close now and don't you uncurl;
Mamma, she's listenin' to that old tune,
Takin' her back to her girlhood and June;
'N' if that ain't a tear, why, I'll bet it's a pearl;
High, baby, ho baby, that's a good girl.

High, baby, ho baby, sleepin' so sweet
While pappy's rubbin' your soft little feet.
When you sing love songs to your little pet,
God grant the tunes do not bring you regret;
'N' God guide your toddlin' coddlin' feet —
High, baby, ho baby, sleepin' so sweet.

(Kansas City Star, July 22, 1894.)

(Untitled)

Where is Boyville? By what track
May we trace our journey back;
Up what mountains, thro' what seas,
By what meadow-lands and leas,
Must we travel to the bourne
Of the shady rows of corn
That lead down to the Willows
Where the day is always morn?

(The Court of Boyville. New York: McClure, Phillips, 1902, ix)

The "Haughty Spirit" in Mr. William

O who is afraid of a bear-skin rug!
    Old dead
      Bear's head!
It couldn't fight back with a lightning bug!
    And Billie says he:
    "Why Geemunee,
It never could lick the left side of a flea!"

But Uncle Lew says bears eat boys whole!
    That's what,
      Blood hot!
And scrunch 'em right down like a grape jelly roll!
    Whee — oo!
    My, what would you do,
If a bear should ever take after you!

Then Billie says Mary's a cowardly calf,
    And doesn't dare
      Touch his hair.

Her sidling up to it would make a dog laugh!
　　　Well gra-shus,
　　　Deary me sus!
For Billie skedaddles before Mary does!

(Undated; William Allen White Library Collection. Reprinted with permission of Barbara White Walker.)

The Truth About the Stork

O the stork stands on the mantel piece with one foot down,
　　　With one foot down,
　　　In an absent-minded frown
O the stork stands on the mantle piece all burnt in brown
　　　Wrapped in a somber meditation;
Now perhaps you think the stork is doing that for fun
　　　Yes that for fun
　　　Well he's not my son
O he's working out his problems and he's carrying one,
　　　For he hasn't got as far as "multiplication!"

(Undated manuscript. William Allen White Collection. Published with permission of Barbara White Walker.)

DEATH

In Remembrance

Sence Idy's Gone

Sence Idy's gone somehow you see
The hours is longer'n they usto be,
An' days an' skies are duller, an' the night
Drips out in oozing seconds drearily
At every hollow clock tick, till the light
Laps up the murky fancies wearily,
An' fever'd dreams 'at come long after dawn
Mix up the happiness I hope to see
'Ith that great sorrow which is haunting me;
'At Idy's gone.

Sence Idy's gone I jist can't stay
In doors; it seems like ev'ry way
I look I find some doin's at 'uz hern:
Her apern mebbe, er the last croshay
She done before she went; at ev'ry turn
I run acrost her mem'ry so's I say
I keep out doors dis kindo's if I's drawn,
An' hang around the crick here ev'ry day,
But even it keeps singun' in its play
'At Idy's gone.

Go into town er to ther store
It's all the same, I hyur the roar
The crick is makun' as it reshes past
The bend; it's sayun' sumpun' more
'N folks believe an' more'n most folks dast,
'Less they believe 'at spirits crosses o'er
An' talks 'ith us; the housework don't git on —
Keeps gittin' tangleder'n 'twas before,
Jist like my head 'at's tangled to the core
Sence Idy's gone.

(*El Dorado Republican,* March 28, 1890; *The Lance,* August 2, 1890; Hattie Horner, *Collections of Kansas Poetry,* 1891.)

After the Funeral

Dist a beginun to notice,
    An' kind a to understand;
Dist a learnun to coo at me an' you,
    An' wave 'ith her little hand.
Seems like she never did cry none
    Ner never uz squawky an' red;
Her smilun is all 'at I ever recall,
    Now 'at the baby's dead.

Dist a beginun to notice,
    An' laff at the dog an' the cat;
An' tryun to say in her sweet baby way
    What she uz tickled at.
Mind how she tried to say mama,
    An' once how we both thought she said:
"Paw"; don't you know I can't make it so —
    An' FEEL 'at the baby's dead.

Dist a beginun to notice,
    An' wantun fer ever to play —
An' that why I guessed 'at Gawd knowed best
    When He came an' took her away.
Fer soon she might notice some sorrow,
    Like me an' her mother's jest had;
Those puore eyes, so blue, might get sin bleared too —
    It's better the baby is dead.

(El Dorado Republican, July 11, 1890.)

A Willer Crick Incident

Long ago before the 'hoppers an' the drouth of semty-four,
Long before we talked of boomin', long before the first Grange store,
Long before they was a city on the banks of Willer Crick,
Come a woman doin' washin' an' a little boy named Dick:
        Kinder weakly like an' sick,
        Wasn't even common quick;
An' the folks said 'at his daddy used to be a loonytic.

He was undersized an' ugly an' was tongue-tied in his talk,
He was awkward an' near-sighted an' he couldn't more'n walk,
An' the other boys all teased him, no one knowed the reason why,
'Cept to hear his mother pet him: "There, ma's angul, there, don' cry."
        When they was nobody nigh
        She would set by him an' sigh,
An' she'd comb his hair an' kiss him: "Ma's boy 'ull be well, by'm bye."

But instead of gettin' stronger Dick grew thinner ev'ry year,
An' although his legs got longer, his pore brain ketched in the gear.
But he always loved the crick so, an' 'twas there 'at he 'u'd play;
Killin' lucky bugs an' buildin' dams 'at always broke away,
        But his mother used to say,
        "God make Dickie strong, some day."
God 'u'd make him strong an' happy, her "pore angul" she 'u'd say.

They was not a long percession when he died, an' all I mind
Was a little green farm wagon with two churs set in behind
But it held a lonely mother sobbin' wildly for her own;
An' the sorrow et in deeper for she knew she grieved alone.
        Mid the sunflow'rs lightly blown,
        Where the sticker weeds are sown,
No one knows the hopes an' heart-aches buried 'neath that rough-
        cut stone.

(*El Dorado Republican,* April 24, 1891; *Current Literature,* VIII (September 1891),
127; *Rhymes by Two Friends,* 153-55; *The Kings and Queens of the Range* (January
15, 1898), 14; Willard Wattles, comp., *Sunflowers: a Book of Kansas Poems,* 61-62).

When the Dead Men Come

The ghost of the Night and the ghost of the Day,
*   And the ghost of the Past that is Dead,*
Are three phantom friends of the Monarch of sleep,
And many a revel these roisterers keep,
A-brewing dream punch that His Highness drinks deep,
*   Till it goes to his somnolent head.*
O the Night's lawless Wine's from the Land of the Dark,
*   Pressed out of the devil's own schemes,*
The Day brings clear water from Things as They Are,
The Past brings its hopes, long since banished afar,
And the drunken god spills over earth from his car,
*   The dead men that come into good women's dreams —*
*   The dead things that come in our dreams.*

Then ho, for the pretty young slip of a wife
    And ho, for the spouse she loves well,
And ho, for the baby she's tucked into bed,
And ho, for the little girl's prayer, she's said;
But alack for the lover she thinks of as dead,
    Alack for the drunken god's spell.
O what is the charm of the Monarch of Sleep,
    And whence are his basilisk[1] beams,
That shine through the curtain of years that are gone,
And turn the wife's face to her womanhood's dawn,
When love was a joy — not a ticket of pawn;
    O why comes the dead to the girl-woman's dreams, —
    The cruel quick dead to her dreams?

And God help her wrestle the wraith[2] of the Night,
    That follows her all through the day;
And God clinch her grip on her heart as they meet —
She and the dead at the turn of the street;
And God bless her husband who sits at her feet,
    And romps with the baby at play.
Then long live the dead that are under the sod;
    Or ride in the sea's shifting streams;

But cursed be the dead things that stay with her yet;
Cursed be the joy that she tries to regret;
Cursed be the mad hour she cannot forget,—
  When the Monarch of sleep spills the dead in her dreams —
   The quick fetid death in her dreams.

Then the over-wrought nerves of the Monarch of Sleep,
  Quiver like lightning at play;
And the mouth of his memory reeks with the bread
That's soured with the wine of a Past that is Dead,
And the fires of remorse in his reeling head,
  Roar through the fever-burned day.
O the Good that men do is Water of Life
  That flows where God's pity bestows.
But the evil men do is all buried to rot,
In the graveyard of life where weeds mark the plot
And the ghouls of regret hover over the spot,
  To dig up the dead that they strew in our dreams
   The dead things that come in our dreams.

(Undated, but typed on White's stationery bearing letterhead of the *Kansas City Journal's* Kansas Bureau office in Topeka, probably dated *ca.* 1891-1892, but remained unpublished. William Allen White Library, Emporia State University, with permission of Barbara White Walker. • 1. A kind of serpent. • 2. An apparition of a living person in his exact likeness, thought to be seen just before his death.)

———

If You Go Away
Roundel

If you go away, a wild Woe will weep o'er the place
Where you sit; she will stretch her stark arms out and sobbingly pray
That Death cool the slow-throbbing pain in her empty embrace —
  If you go away.

Perhaps it is better to go ere you tire of the play —
Ere the hulls of your hopes are torn open to leave bitter trace
Of the worm — when your hopes are first blushing and ere they decay.

I know it is hard to be still and look Death in the face;
With lips sweet and dewy from Life's morning kisses to say:
I am ready. But God! 't will be harder to keep in the race —
     If you go away.

(Agora II, July 1892, 62; *Rhymes by Two Friends,* 225-56; J.H. Powers, *Some Emporia Verse.)*

Out in the Dark

Dear, I must go.
The old clock says it: nine — ten — hark!
    Of course the old clock can not know
    That every hour-beat is a blow
    Upon my heart — I love you so.
    Some day we'll taunt the old clock though —
Dear, I must go — out in the dark.

Out in the dark,
Where, on the night wind sweet I throw
    A kiss my love guides to its mark;
    And where each mellow heav'nly spark
    Joins in a love song that the lark
    Translates at morn; where dreams embark —
Out in the dark — dear, I must go.

Dear, I must go,
For God hath willed it, loved one, hark!
    And he alone can truly know
    How crushed and bruised beneath His blow
    Our hearts are, for we love love so —
    Some day we'll triumph o'er Death though —
Dear, I must go — out in the dark.

Out in the dark,
Where hov'ring near you I shall throw
    My love about you, and you'll mark

My presence by the glowing spark
That mem'ry breathes on; th' meadow lark —
At dusk will call you to embark —
Out in the dark, dear, I must go.

L'ENVOI

Hold to my hand, dear heart, for oh,
  I am so weak, yes, dear, blind — stark;
And God — I do not want to go
  Out in the dark.

(Kansas City Star, November 17, 1892; *Rhymes by Two Friends,* 227-28; J.H. Powers, *Some Emporia Verse.)*

Alone!

A woman's soul winged thro' the sky,
  Quitting this poor clay burr,
      And three there were
      Who promised her
To wait until she came by.

And one of the men she had loved in youth,
  And one bore a husband's name,
      And one brought shame
      To her life when he came,
And loosened her hands with truth.

Then her soul shrank back in a ghastly groan,
  At the thought of her near Disgrace.
      There was not one face,
      At the meeting place,—
And she shivered on all alone.

(Kansas City Star, February 21, 1894.)

One With Nature

Oh God, when life shall throw aside
    The husk of my identity;
    Worn sere[1] and useless — when in Thee
My soul shall melt as on a tide,
    Let me revisit earth's dull plane
    Wearing the spirit of the rain.

Then shall the songs I cannot sing
    With this imperfect voice of clay
    Find utterance; and then I may
Strike surely every vibrant string —
    The chords of love, of joy, of dole[2] —
    That wakes an echo in the soul.

Youth shall hear glory on my breath
    And Age, sweet solace, grief tears;
    And widowed hearts that sob o'er biers
Through me shall know the sham[3] of death.
    Oh spirit of the rain to be
    What Blessed immortality.

(Undated, holograph. William Allen White Library, Emporia State University. Printed with permission of Barbara White Walker. • 1. Dried up; withered. • 2. Grief. • 3. False; feigned.)

———————

Protean Death

There lived a life; Death took all save the clay.
    There lived a hope; Death took all save the shell
    Of crumbled memories here where it fell.
Why should we dread that Death which steals away
A life, yet smile to see a hope decay?
    'Twas real Death smote the hope, who rang the knell
    And bade us weep for life; the self-same spell
That now stills life we laughed at yesterday.

(*Emporia Gazette,* undated. William Allen White Library, Emporia State University, with permission of Barbara White Walker.)

The Punctilious Guest

The wedding will wait till the morrow,
    Ruddy Joy's ever ready to play ;
Approacheth proud ashen-faced sorrow?
    Thou must go and meet her to-day.

(Undated, William Allen White Library, Emporia State University. Printed with permission of Barbara White Walker.)

———————

Where Is Thy Victory?

Communion? — yes, death, lonely death has its vanities
    Here in the graveyard has envy gone daft
There's a new, modish, smart square block of granite is
    Lording it over this clean marble shaft.
Yonder poor, slanting, thin slab — what a bant[1] it is
    Under, all moss-fouled, all jeered at and chaffed.

So are the graves — preened in blue grass and terraces,
    Meek under wild turf, or sunken in shame.
Even the coffins for outcasts or heiresses
    Proud steel or poor pine, mark great or ill fame.
Lord, should not men escape castes, cults and heresies
    Here at the end of life's curious game?

When in the earth I shall close a strange history
    When I shall shuck off this husk of my soul,
When on a pure star another than this story
    Starts in new runes[2] on an unsullied scroll,
When I shall fathom some of God's mystery —
    Build me no wall, 'gainst the worm and the mole.

Bar not brothers who take but a part of me

Back to the sunshine, though low my rebirth.
I would not lie there steel-bound while the heart of me
    Yearns to be flesh, bone or nerves upon earth.
Let me come back e'er the times get a start of me
    Though I must rise through the worm's narrow girth.

I would feel life's thrill, what e'er fate may swallow me
    In a wide cycle where ever life goes.
Who'd be a clod in the tomb of a Ptolemy
    If he could blush as a sensitive rose.
O let me throb yet where youth's joy may follow me
    In some mad blood when the hyacinth blows.

Block, shaft or slab, matters not when one thinks of it
    Terrace, or wild turf or weed-tangled square,
If the life chain shall reach — who cares what links of it —
    Creeping or crawling, forbidding or fair.
Life — how one drinks of it — hones[3] for the stinks of it —
    Only to pulse in the sunshine and air!

(Unpublished, signed typescript located in the William Allen White Library, Emporia State University, with permission of Barbara White Walker. The typescript includes date of December 17, 1913. • 1. Act of sharing, participation. • 2. Alphabetic characters used by Teutonic and Germanic peoples from about the third century A.D. • 3. To grumble or lament.)

A Song of the Night Wind

The wind in the gray of the prairie moon
    Breathes a long, trembling, sorrowing sigh;
Eerie and tender — a soft lullabye,
    Such as a mother's sad heart would croon,
To a babe that would never cry.

The plumes of the poplars are bowed with grief;
    Sadly the maple trees whisper of woe;
Gently its sobs through the long grasses go;
    My heart keeps time with the tree and the leaf,
Whose secrets I cannot know.

Maybe they mourn for the dead that mould,
    Under the roll of our hurrying feet —
Dead who were happy when life was sweet —
    Dead, who here oft to the night wind told,
Vain hopes while their pulses beat.

Maybe some dreamer in other years,
    Will stand o'er the spot where my dust may life,
And hark to the night wind's hopeless cry
    And feel in his glad heart the rush of tears —
    And wonder and wonder why.

(Unpublished manuscript, typed and signed, located in the William Allen White Library, Emporia State University. Permission to publish given by Barbara White Walker.)